**INTERNATIONAL
ENERGY AGENCY**

POWER
GENERATION
INVESTMENT
IN ELECTRICITY
MARKETS

9267754

INTERNATIONAL ENERGY AGENCY
9, rue de la Fédération,
75739 Paris Cedex 15, France

ORGANISATION FOR ECONOMIC CO-OPERATION AND DEVELOPMENT

The International Energy Agency (IEA) is an autonomous body which was established in November 1974 within the framework of the Organisation for Economic Co-operation and Development (OECD) to implement an international energy programme.

It carries out a comprehensive programme of energy co-operation among twenty-six* of the OECD's thirty member countries. The basic aims of the IEA are:

- to maintain and improve systems for coping with oil supply disruptions;

- to promote rational energy policies in a global context through co-operative relations with non-member countries, industry and international organisations;

- to operate a permanent information system on the international oil market;

- to improve the world's energy supply and demand structure by developing alternative energy sources and increasing the efficiency of energy use;

- to assist in the integration of environmental and energy policies.

IEA member countries: Australia, Austria, Belgium, Canada, the Czech Republic, Denmark, Finland, France, Germany, Greece, Hungary, Ireland, Italy, Japan, the Republic of Korea, Luxembourg, the Netherlands, New Zealand, Norway, Portugal, Spain, Sweden, Switzerland, Turkey, the United Kingdom, the United States. The European Commission also takes part in the work of the IEA.

Pursuant to Article 1 of the Convention signed in Paris on 14th December 1960, and which came into force on 30th September 1961, the Organisation for Economic Co-operation and Development (OECD) shall promote policies designed:

- to achieve the highest sustainable economic growth and employment and a rising standard of living in member countries, while maintaining financial stability, and thus to contribute to the development of the world economy;

- to contribute to sound economic expansion in member as well as non-member countries in the process of economic development; and

- to contribute to the expansion of world trade on a multilateral, non-discriminatory basis in accordance with international obligations.

The original member countries of the OECD are Austria, Belgium, Canada, Denmark, France, Germany, Greece, Iceland, Ireland, Italy, Luxembourg, the Netherlands, Norway, Portugal, Spain, Sweden, Switzerland, Turkey, the United Kingdom and the United States. The following countries became members subsequently through accession at the dates indicated hereafter: Japan (28th April 1964), Finland (28th January 1969), Australia (7th June 1971), New Zealand (29th May 1973), Mexico (18th May 1994), the Czech Republic (21st December 1995), Hungary (7th May 1996), Poland (22nd November 1996), the Republic of Korea (12th December 1996) and Slovakia (28th September 2000). The Commission of the European Communities takes part in the work of the OECD (Article 13 of the OECD Convention).

FOREWORD

Electricity policy in OECD countries over the past decade has been focused on the liberalisation of electricity markets. In doing so, governments have shifted the responsibility for financing investment in power generation away from generally state-owned monopolies to private investors. No longer able to automatically pass on costs to consumers, and with future prices of electricity uncertain, investors face a much riskier environment for power generation investment decisions.

Governments have remained concerned about the adequacy and the composition of power generation investment in a liberalised market. Previous IEA work has found that in most markets which were opened to competition, the level of investment in generating capacity has been adequate. This report looks at how internalising the risks of investment has changed the investors and the composition of investments. The report finds that while capital and total costs remain the fundamental parameters shaping investment choices, technologies which can be installed quickly and operated flexibly in response to markets are increasingly attractive. Power firms are also responding to the uncertain environment by finding ways to mitigate their investment risks, by greater use of contracting, by acquiring retail businesses, and through mergers with natural gas supply businesses.

Relying on market prices to signal the need for new power generation investment and to stimulate a timely reaction of the investors, particularly for peaking capacity, has introduced a new challenge for governments. While liberalisation was expected to limit government intervention in the electricity market, volatile electricity prices, signalling the need for greater capacity, have raised prices to consumers and put pressure on governments to intervene. This study looks at several cases of volatile prices in IEA electricity markets, the governments' responses to these prices and the implications for investment in power generation, particularly in peak capacity. It finds that market prices can be a sufficient incentive for new investment in peak capacity, and that government intervention into the market only to limit prices may undermine such investment.

Yet there remains much for governments to do. It is vital that governments define the roles of all players in reformed electricity markets as clearly as possible. For governments, that means establishing the policies and leaving their implementation to regulatory authorities, and the pricing and the reaction to prices to the market players. In particular, it is for governments to define their objectives for the electricity sector, and for the regulator to design the rules, so that sufficient production capacity − or responsive demand − can be properly financed, with an adequate return on investment. In addition, governments should ensure that, when a decision to invest is taken, its implementation is not delayed by excessive or inappropriate authorisation procedures. More importantly, to attract investment, governments must maintain their commitment to ensuring the success of the market, and not reverse direction under the pressure of price hikes or other unpleasant surprises along the way. Certainty over the direction that legislation will take is one of the most important preconditions for investors.

This book is part of the IEA series on electricity market reform. It is published under my authority as Executive Director of the International Energy Agency.

Claude Mandil
Executive Director

ACKNOWLEDGEMENTS

The principal author of this report is Peter Fraser of the Energy Diversification Division, working under the direction of Ralf Dickel, Head of Division, and Noé van Hulst, Director of the Office for Long Term Co-operation and Policy Analysis.

This book has benefited greatly from the papers presented at an IEA/NEA workshop, "Power Generation Investment in Liberalised Electricity Markets" held at the IEA on 25-26 March 2003. The comments received from the IEA's Standing Committee on Long Term Co-operation, Doug Cooke and Maria Argiri from the IEA Secretariat, John Paffenbarger of Constellation Energy, and Dean Travers of Electrabel have all been very helpful.

TABLE OF CONTENTS

LIST OF TABLES

LIST OF FIGURES

EXECUTIVE SUMMARY

Electricity markets have been opened to competition in nearly all IEA countries. The introduction of competition in the generation and retail supply of electricity should improve the economic efficiency of the power sector. There is a great deal of evidence to suggest that market liberalisation has generally improved the productive efficiency of the sector. Furthermore, with many markets opened in the presence of surpluses of generating capacity, competitive pressures have reduced power prices.

The key long-term question for improving the economic efficiency of the electricity sector is whether investment performance in power generation will improve. Much of the focus has been on whether the overall level of investment in generating capacity has been adequate to ensure security of electricity supply. Previous IEA work[1] has shown substantial investment in power generation has taken place and that OECD electricity markets generally provide reliable electricity supply with the exception of California notwithstanding[2]. However, it also concluded that the biggest challenges remain ahead – most markets are just beginning to approach their first major investment cycle as surplus capacity is absorbed.

This report examines three other major issues associated with power generation investment in liberalised electricity markets. The first issue is how liberalisation and investment risk have affected technology choices in power generation. In particular, given the anticipated growth in investment in natural gas-fired power generation, it asks whether "short-termism" by investors is undermining an economically rational allocation of capital. Chapter 2 examines the risks that investors in power generation face in liberalised markets.

The second issue addressed is how power generation investors are adapting to investment risks. Financial hedges have not developed

---

1. Security of Supply in Electricity Markets: Evidence and Policy Issues, *International Energy Agency, Paris 2002.*

2. *This report also concluded that existing transmission interconnection capacity was insufficient, and there was a need for policies to encourage such investment.*

sufficiently to offer significant long-term hedging value to investors. As a consequence, firms are seeking to hedge these risks by the use of long-term contracts, by integration of generation with retail, by growing in size, and by mergers between gas and electricity companies. Chapter 3 looks at these strategies and discusses whether such structural changes are consistent with efficient energy markets.

The emergence of tighter electricity markets has led to increased electricity price volatility. Increased price volatility has put pressure on governments to intervene in electricity markets. The report reviews recent cases of electricity price volatility in Norway, Canada, Australia and New Zealand and discusses the impact of the governments' response to these crises on the prospects for efficient new generation investment.

Risk and its Influence on Power Generation Investment and Corporate Structure

The reform of electricity and gas markets has led to major changes in the way decisions are taken on power sector investment. Opening the sector to competition has led to the internalisation of risk in investment decision-making. Investors now examine power generation options according to the different financial risks posed by the different technologies.

Given the long-term nature of electricity investments, investment decisions in baseload generating capacity are being made on the basis of long-term fundamentals rather than looking at short-term behaviour in the spot or forward electricity markets. Conventional discounted cash flow methods are still most often used. Nevertheless, investors are beginning to take account of differences in risk levels in assessing the likely profitability of different investments.

The current market preference for gas-fired power generation for baseload generation in many OECD countries can be explained mainly by the perceived lower cost of gas-fired generation. The characteristics of the combined cycle gas turbine (CCGT), its low capital cost, and its flexibility have also added to its attractiveness. The importance of CCGT means that gas markets assume a greater importance than ever for power generation development. For governments, this means moving forward on liberalisation, and monitoring investment in both gas and electric infrastructure.

The preference for gas-fired power generation does expose investors to increased fuel price risk. The creation or development of electricity and natural gas markets has led to a system where, in the absence of hedging possibilities, price risks cannot be managed, but must be assessed by probabilistic approaches.

Nuclear plants can be financed in an electricity market, but this will be much easier if customers share the risks. The decision of Finland's TVO company, a large electricity co-operative (see Chapter 3), to proceed with the investment in a nuclear plant is the first by a company in a competitive electricity market. The structure of the investment is exceptional, however, with large consumers of electricity willing to take the risks of investing in a nuclear plant because they expect to be able to obtain the long-term financial benefits.

The adequacy of investment in peaking generation remains an even more sensitive issue. The low numbers of hours of operation of peaking plant have led some to question whether markets can bring forward adequate peaking capacity. Low capital and high flexibility in operation are particularly important attributes in attempting to value peaking capacity. While investors have long been aware of the qualitative benefits of flexibility in a liberalised market, new techniques have now been developed to quantify the value of flexibility. In particular, they suggest that flexible peaking capacity may be much more profitable than traditional approaches would predict.

The current economic downturn in the US electricity market has lenders looking for strong companies with stable revenue flows and customer bases for future investments. Liberalisation has also affected the way power plants are financed. Early enthusiasm for the merchant power plant model, where power plants are financed without the security of regulated profits, has dissipated thanks to adverse investment experience in the United States.

Hedging Risk in Power Generation Investment

Firms are also seeking new strategies to hedge their investments. The absence of liquidity in financial markets for electricity and for natural gas, particularly for longer-term products, means that investors must seek other means of hedging their electricity price (and fuel price) risks. Longer-term contracts for electricity between producers and retailers help both manage price volatility. There has also been increased merger activity between generators and retailers in several markets. Mergers between electricity and gas producers are partially motivated by increased opportunities for arbitrage.

Power generating companies are also growing in size, in part to be able to finance more of their investment on their own balance sheets. These mergers are increasing concerns about the potential impacts on competition in electricity markets and can be expected to continue to attract close regulatory attention.

Electricity Markets, Electricity Price Volatility and Investment

Chapter 4 examines recent price crises in Australia (South Australia), Canada (Ontario and Alberta), Norway and New Zealand. Drawing general lessons from government management of electricity "price crises" and its impact on investment is difficult given the rather different circumstances of each crisis and the relatively short period of time that has passed. Nevertheless, some observations can be made on each case.

The experience in Australia, where investment response has been in the face of robust growth in demand, suggests that governments need to carefully consider the implications of their policies and subsequent actions on private investors that the reforms are attempting to attract. If investors expect that governments will intervene in wholesale markets to prevent prices from rising to sufficiently high levels to recover costs of peaking capacity, then attracting that investment will become more difficult and hence undermine reliability objectives. The experience in South Australia suggests that markets can respond to price signals and meet demand and reliability requirements where government policies are consistent with the development of efficient and sustainable electricity markets, and where they are implemented transparently and consistently.

The Canadian experience with retail price caps appears to be yielding two very different results in terms of investment. The Alberta market experience suggests that a sufficiently high cap on prices may not deter investment in new capacity. However, the recent experience in Ontario shows that actions by government to intervene with low price caps can deter investment. Indeed, such political intervention destroys the integrity of the market – by destroying incentives to invest and by creating moral hazard. If generators believe that customers will be protected by government intervention from spikes that are needed to recover fixed costs, then markets will fail to deliver new capacity.

This is not to suggest that price caps may be needed in wholesale markets at any time. When there is a demonstration of market power being exercised, as was seen in the California market, price caps may be needed as a temporary instrument to prevent excessive profits from being taken. However, such a measure should be transitional only, and should be phased out as quickly as other mechanisms to address market power, such as enhanced demand response, can be implemented.

By contrast, the New Zealand situation presents quite unusual circumstances, because the combination of its heavy reliance on hydro resources and its lack of interconnection with other non-hydro systems makes it vulnerable to energy shortages that are difficult to predict. Having otherwise surplus capacity available for infrequent dry years does not appear to be economic.

The government proposal to contract for reserve capacity that would be set aside from the market and be offered only during dry years would address this problem. The main difficulty with this proposal is the terms under which the capacity would be released to the market. The government has stated that it intends to release the capacity in the market only during times of shortage. It will, however, be difficult to define the level of shortage and the quantity to be released in a way that does not influence the behaviour of market participants. Disruption would be minimised if the capacity were only to be made available at very high prices. But there will be pressure on the government to release capacity to the market whenever prices rise. In this regard, the situation would be analogous to those pressures on IEA member governments to release oil stocks to the market.

In Norway, the government faced considerable dissatisfaction with high electricity prices. However, there were at least three factors that helped give the government greater confidence to rely on market mechanisms to resolve the crisis. First, there had been a long history of open electricity markets in Norway, a result which had led to a better utilisation of generating capacity and lower electricity prices over several years. The fact that customers had already enjoyed several years of benefits increased confidence that the electricity markets do create benefits for end consumers. Second, the opening of the market internationally, thereby getting access to additional supplies from neighbouring countries, helped to reduce the risk that the market could be manipulated when capacity was tight. Finally, the existence of the international electricity market also meant that effective intervention by government would have to be co-ordinated with action by the governments of the other countries served by this market. In fact, such co-ordinated discussions among Nordic ministers are carried out on a regular basis. This mechanism is much better suited to considered joint action rather than a short-term response.

Thus, while electricity markets may be delivering adequate levels of investment, price spikes are testing government commitment to allow markets to sort things out. Concentration of electricity markets and concerns about the manipulation of prices in some markets, such as California, make it difficult for a government or a regulatory body to determine if prices are reflecting scarcity or are the result of the exercise of market power. In some cases, particularly when smaller consumers are exposed to these price spikes, this has sparked government intervention in electricity markets.

Protection of consumers from high prices must be carefully designed to avoid disruption of the market. Intervention by governments in the electricity markets can create regulatory uncertainty which can discourage investors. Thus, interventions such as default supply options for small consumers should be chosen carefully, with an awareness of the risks involved. Price caps, if employed, should be set before spikes occur, and at sufficiently high levels. They should also be transitional measures until a more workably competitive market can be established. Governments must also work in co-operation with governments of interconnected markets to ensure that measures do not work at cross purposes.

Addressing the very high price volatility experienced in electricity markets is most efficiently done by addressing its cause: the very low demand-price elasticity of electricity consumption. There is considerable evidence that this elasticity is lower than it could be because of the lack of ability and incentives for demand to respond to price. Enhancing demand response will reduce the extreme prices experienced during tight supply, in effect by widening the price peaks over a larger number of hours. This will create a more stable environment for power generation investment and should increase confidence that electricity markets can be used to ration capacity by price, ensuring that the supply of electricity remains reliable.

Price volatility also raises questions about the market's ability to ensure a secure and reliable supply. Attracting sufficient investment should not be a problem in OECD countries since consumers place very high value on electricity and pay cost-recovering prices. The difficulty is really finding a model that properly values the security of the electricity supply. The old monopoly system worked but at the cost of losing economic efficiency. A new system based on bilateral contracts between producers and consumers can also work, but consumers need to place a value on their security of supply. For large consumers, this is not a problem, but the issue for small consumers is less clear, since consumers may be less aware of the price risks. Governments have a role in making consumers aware of these risks.

As a consequence, the government's security of supply policy is tied up with its policies affecting new investment. Some measures can be taken, for example, to remove obstacles to new investment by streamlining approval of new generating plant.

However, mechanisms that intervene directly in electricity markets, such as capacity market mechanisms, can have much stronger effects on the cost of electricity. Several governments have recently reviewed capacity mechanisms and have rejected their use because they expected such mechanisms would increase the cost of electricity and they questioned the effectiveness of these mechanisms at stimulating new investment. Nevertheless, a well-designed capacity mechanism that requires retailers to have arranged adequate resources during peak periods might help provide incentives for retailers to acquire sufficient peak capacity (or to work with customers to have sufficient demand response).

The report has the following five recommendations:

- **Define clearly the government's role in electricity market reform and the terms of its involvement as precisely as possible.** Attracting investment in power generation requires a clear market design, with predictable changes and no interference into the market or into the operation of the independent institutions established to implement the market reform. The government's role must be clearly set out both as the agent of the reforms and in its energy policy involvement once the market opens.

- **Recognise that electricity price fluctuations are intrinsic to well-functioning electricity markets.** Allowing markets to signal the need for new investment in generation means that prices will go high on occasion. Governments need to anticipate that such fluctuations will occur and ensure that consumers are aware of price risks and have options to mitigate these risks.

- **Develop demand response within electricity markets.** Fluctuating spot electricity prices offer rewards as well as risks. The low price elasticity of electricity demand, especially for small customers, is at least partly due to the inability to reward consumers for adjusting their consumption when prices are high. Greater demand response in electricity markets is needed to help ensure that electricity markets are always able to clear, i.e. by rationing electricity supply according to price rather than through brownouts or blackouts. A stronger demand response will help mitigate market power in electricity markets and provide potential investors with more predictable energy (and ancillary service) prices and therefore decrease investment risks.

■ **Be prepared to detect and to act upon wholesale electricity market manipulation.** In order to address concerns about wholesale electricity market manipulation, governments must ensure that electricity markets have monitoring mechanisms that can not only detect manipulation as it is occurring but also take prompt action to mitigate its impacts. This will reduce pressure on the government to respond e.g. through direct price caps which could drive away needed investment.

■ **Monitoring adequacy of gas markets and investments.** The preference of investors in some markets for CCGT for building new power generating capacity means that gas markets assume a greater importance than ever for power generation development. For governments, this means moving forward on liberalisation of both the gas market and the electricity market, and monitoring the adequacy of investment in both gas and electric infrastructure.

INTRODUCTION

Electricity markets are opening to competition in nearly all IEA countries. Most IEA member governments have implemented laws to liberalise wholesale electricity markets and allow at least some of the large consumers the opportunity to choose suppliers, to permit electricity generators and consumers to have non-discriminatory access to transmission and distribution systems, to liberalise electricity trading on a bilateral basis and on organised exchanges, and to allow for free entry of new producers, on non-discriminatory conditions.

The main objective of electricity market liberalisation is to improve the economic efficiency of the electricity supply industry. The introduction of competition in the generation and retail supply of electricity is expected to improve productive efficiency by reducing operating costs and improving allocative efficiency by aligning prices with costs.

There is a great deal of evidence to suggest that market liberalisation has, in general, led to a reduction in operating costs of generating plants by improving labour productivity, reducing maintenance costs and improving fuel purchasing strategies[3]. As a number of electricity markets have been opened in the presence of surplus generating capacity, there have been very strong competitive pressures to reduce such costs as prices have fallen. Indeed, all evidence indicates that such cost reductions are occurring, and that firms are becoming more efficient in response to price signals.

As a capital-intensive industry, a key sign of an efficiently functioning electricity supply industry is an efficient allocation of capital. Previous IEA work[4], *Security of Supply in Electricity Markets: Evidence and Policy Issues*, examined the question of the adequacy of the investment levels in seven reformed markets. Its main conclusions are:

■ Substantial investment has taken place since market liberalisation and OECD electricity markets are generally reliable, the exception of California notwithstanding.

---

3. See, for example, IEA, 1999.

4. IEA, 2002a.

- Reserve margins have fallen generally, consistent with the improvement of allocative efficiency.

- New capacity investment favoured the most economic option: natural gas where this was available but also coal where this option was less expensive.

- It was too early to conclude whether electricity generation investment would mimic "boom and bust" cycles observed in other industries.

- Markets may increase flexibility of the demand side (e.g. through load-shifting or distributed generation) which would reduce the size of the reserve capacity required.

- The biggest challenges remain ahead – most markets are just beginning to approach their first major investment cycle[5].

However, the overall level of investment is but one of the major issues surrounding power generation investment in liberalised markets. A recent IEA study has looked at the level of investment required and how this investment will be attracted to the power market. It concludes that the power sector of OECD countries will need $4 trillion of investment between 2000 and 2030. About half this amount would be needed for power generation investment[6].

This report will focus on three other issues. The first is the impact of liberalisation on power generation investors and on the technologies chosen for investment. It will consider how investors have adapted to the market in terms of their analytical methods and their corporate structures in response to the greatly increased risks that need to be borne. It will then consider the consequences of these changes for the choice of power generation technology for investment.

Investment in global power generation has been growing strongly. Figure 1 shows the global orders for new power plants since the 1950s, with orders for gas turbines shown separately starting in 1991. It shows

---

5. IEA, 2002a also examined the question of transmission investment and concluded that there was a need for policies to encourage investment in transmission in many OECD regions, a message reinforced by the blackout in the United States and Canada in August 2003. The present report is focused strictly on investment in power generation.

6. IEA, 2003a.

Global Power Generation Orders, Including Gas Turbines (1950-2003)

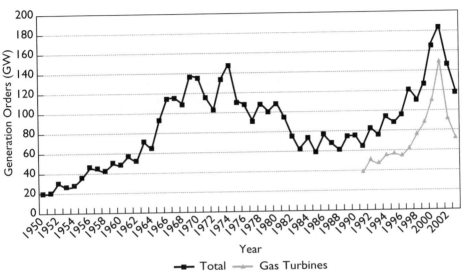

Year

■ Total ──── Gas Turbines

Source: Siemens Power Generation (2003 is estimated).

a steady growth trend with two boom periods – one from the mid-1960s until the early 1980s and a much shorter boom in the late 1990s that peaked in 2001.

The figure also shows the emerging role that natural gas-fired turbines have come to play in power generation, accounting for 65% of the capacity ordered since 1991. While this emergence is partly due to improvements in gas-fired generation technology, there is no question that in many liberalised markets gas-fired generation has been favoured.

This preference for natural gas-fired generation is expected to continue into the future. The 2002 *World Energy Outlook* (WEO) suggests that, given current policies, over half of the 2 000 GW of generating capacity added between 1999 and 2030 in the OECD will use natural gas (Figure 2).

The strong preference for gas-fired power generation has raised concerns about energy diversification. The reason for this is that, as

Figure 2

Share of Projected Capacity Additions in OECD Generating Capacity by Fuel (1999-2030)

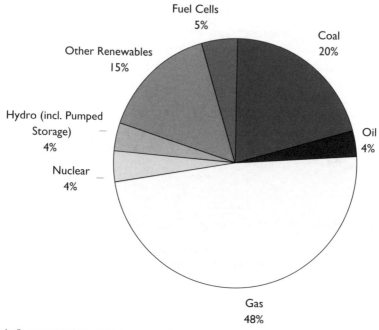

Note: Fuel cells are accounted separately but are assumed to use natural gas.
Source: IEA, 2002b.

shown in the *World Energy Outlook 2002*, the increased demand for electric power is the main driver for investment in all commercial primary energies but oil. Therefore, the expectation that power generation markets in the OECD will be increasingly attracted to natural gas will have a real influence on the primary energy mix and on the diversity of electricity supply, more than doubling its share to 32% of the 2030 fuel mix.

The issue to be addressed is whether these investments are consistent with economic efficiency or whether "short-termism" on the part of investors in liberalised markets is leading to decisions that are inconsistent with an economically rational allocation of capital. Chapter 2 will examine how investors have adapted to reformed electricity markets through the need to internalise various investment risks in their decision-making. It discusses the nature of the risks that now need to be internalised and compares qualitatively the risk attributes of different power generation technologies. It will discuss the new techniques for quantification of such risks, and the implications of the results of such analyses for investors. It will examine the consequences on the choice of technologies for power generation.

The second issue is how power generation investors are adapting to investment risks. At the time of market liberalisation, it was argued that the development of financial instruments would help investors by providing financial hedges for future electricity or gas prices. In fact, such markets have been slow to develop and appear unlikely to offer long-term financial hedges that might offset price and fuel cost risks. As a consequence, firms are seeking to hedge these risks by the use of long-term contracts, by integration of generation with retail, by growing in size, and by mergers between gas and electricity companies. Chapter 3 will look at these strategies and discuss whether such structural changes are consistent with efficient energy markets.

The third major issue to be addressed in the study is inspired by recent developments in several OECD electricity markets. During the past two years, markets in Australia, New Zealand, Canada and Scandinavia have all experienced electricity price spikes. The tendency of deregulated power markets to produce price spikes can – depending on market design and consumers' choices – significantly raise bills for small consumers. This has in turn created what can be termed an electricity "price crisis" and pushed the issue to the top of the agenda of the governments concerned. Table 1 summarises the major crises in several jurisdictions.

The causes of crises are varied. Unlike California, market manipulation or bad market design does not appear to have played a significant role in the other cases. Like California, governments in all these markets have been placed under considerable political pressure to respond to the concerns of consumers about prices and the security of supply.

These electricity "price crises" and the governments' responses to them are critical to understand the future of using spot prices in electricity markets to signal the need for new investment. Chapter 4 will briefly

Table 1

Summary of Markets Experiencing Electricity "Price Crises"

Jurisdiction	Cause of Price Crisis	Duration
California	Tight capacity (low rainfall), manipulated markets	5/2000 – 5/2001
Canada (Alberta)	High fuel prices, high electricity prices in neighbouring markets	9/2000 – 3/2001
New Zealand	Tight energy supply due to low rainfall and concerns about availability of thermal fuels	4/2001 – 7/2001 4/2003 – 6/2003
Australia (South Australia)	Tight capacity due to rapid growth	1/2002 -3/2002
Nord Pool	Tight energy supply due to low rainfall/cold winter	12/2002 – 03/2003
Canada (Ontario)	Demand growth, delay in capacity investment	7/2002 – 7/2003

examine price crises in Canada, Australia, New Zealand and Norway, and discuss how the governments' responses will affect future investment.

Chapter 5 will summarise the main conclusions of the report and offer policy recommendations.

RISK AND POWER GENERATION INVESTMENT

Introduction

Prior to the liberalisation of energy markets, energy firms were able to operate as integrated monopolies able to pass on all costs of investments to energy consumers. For example, in the electric power sector, utilities could expect the cost of their prudently incurred investments in power generation, including an adequate rate of return, to be recovered from consumers. In view of that guaranteed rate of return, utilities could finance their investment with a low share of equity and borrow at interest rates close to government debt yields. There was no market risk. The main risk was the risk of unfavourable regulatory decisions and cost overruns due to bad project management. Overinvestment could be accommodated as excess reserve margin since excess capacity did not create a reduction in electricity prices.

In such an environment, most of the risks associated with such investments were not directly a concern of the energy company. Increased costs, if demonstrated to be prudently incurred, could be passed on as increased prices. There was little incentive for companies to take account of such risks when making investment decisions.

The introduction of liberalisation in energy markets is removing the regulatory risk shield and exposing investors to various risks or exposing them to risks in different ways. Generators are no longer guaranteed the ability to recover all costs from power consumers. Nor is the future price level guaranteed.

The issue of interest here is how the internalisation of risks affects decision-making on investment. This chapter discusses new techniques for quantification of such risks, and the implications of the results of such analyses for investors. It will examine the consequences on the choice of technologies for power generation, and how the structure of firms is changing in response to perceived risk.

Power Generation Investment Risks in the Liberalised Market

Investment in power generation comprises a large and diverse set of risks. Business risks include:

- Economy-wide factors that affect the demand for electricity or the availability of labour and capital.

- Factors under the control of the policy-makers, such as regulatory (economic and non-economic) and political risks, with possible implications for costs, financing conditions and on earnings.

- Factors under the control of the company, such as the size and diversity of its investment programme, the choice and diversity of generation technologies, control of costs during construction and operation.

- The price and volume risks in the electricity market.

- Fuel price and, to a lesser extent, availability risks.

- Financial risks arising from the financing of investment. They can to some extent be mitigated by the capital structure of the company[7].

The level of risk anticipated by an investor in a power plant will be reflected in the level of return expected on that investment. The greater the business and financial risks, the higher the return that will be demanded.

The most fundamental change affecting the value of investments in liberalised markets is the inherent uncertainty about electricity prices in electricity markets. The uncertain future level of prices from investment in generation creates a risk for the investor. While this risk affects all generating technologies[8], it does so in different ways. Technologies which have a higher specific investment for capacity even though they may have relatively low fuel costs (wind, nuclear) are more greatly affected by this risk because there is less they can do to respond. Thus, although high capital cost and low fuel cost technologies will likely be competitive in the

---

7. IEA, 1994.

8. Conversely, if e.g. renewable energy technologies are favoured by long-term contracts at fixed prices, this significantly reduces this risk compared to technologies that would need to take an uncertain market price.

short-run and therefore produce electricity, they will be more exposed to cover capital employed. A firm reliant on such technologies may find itself in financial difficulties if prices slump for a prolonged period. The recent experience of British Energy in the UK electricity market – leading to action by the UK government to support the company – is a case in point[9].

Uncertain electricity prices also expose projects that have a long lead and construction time to additional risks. Economies of scale favour large power projects over small ones as capital costs per kW for a given technology generally decrease with increasing scale, or at least appear to do so. However, the combination of a long lead time, uncertain growth in demand for electricity and price, and uncertainty in the total cost of financing construction increase risks for larger projects. Furthermore, very large projects that must effectively be built as a single large plant (e.g. a very large hydro dam) are more vulnerable to this type of risk than projects for which development can be phased in as several smaller power plants in response to market conditions.

The cost of fuel can be a significant additional risk to profits, particularly for technologies where fuel costs are a high proportion of total generating costs. Natural gas technologies are particularly sensitive to fuel prices and price volatility, as fuel costs tend to constitute the majority of generating costs.

Uncertainty in future natural gas prices is increased by the liberalisation of the natural gas market, and the disappearance of long-term contracts available for the supply of natural gas for power generation. High volatility of natural gas prices also will tend to increase short-term risks associated with natural gas. If rises in natural gas prices accompany falls in electricity prices, and the generator has not financed the project in recognition of this risk, the financial distress for natural gas power generators can be severe. A number of cogeneration facilities in the Netherlands found themselves in precisely this situation – leading to action by the Netherlands government to support cogeneration[10].

---

9. *Hewitt, 2002.*

10. *IEA, 2002c, p. 63.*

The situation for investors is further complicated by the outlook for resource availability and cost. Although sufficient economic resources exist for natural gas and other fuels used in power generation[11], sufficient investment is needed in infrastructure to produce and transport fuels to power plants. A further consideration is the source of the future gas supplies. The source of natural gas supplies is expected to shift strongly over the next 30 years, resulting in a quadrupling of OECD natural gas import volumes, and increased reliance on production from outside the OECD[12]. While resource rents from the development of existing domestic natural gas resources or from gas imports from IEA countries have been relatively predictable, rent-seeking by non-IEA gas-producing countries may be a significant long-term uncertainty.

The key question for an investor in fossil-fired power generation in an open market will be the level and development of the difference between the price of electricity and the cost of fuel used to produce it – the so-called "spark spread". The importance of the spark spread will depend on the type of power plant and how it is intended to be used. For baseload power plants, a relatively large favourable spark spread is desirable so that the plant can operate at all times to recover the specifically higher capital costs of such a plant over a large number of hours. For peaking load plants, with higher fuel costs, capital costs must be recouped over a smaller number of hours. Thus, peaking plant characteristics will favour a flexible generating plant that is able to take advantage whenever the spark spread is favourable. This requires not only technical flexibility to respond to changing prices, but, in the case of natural gas, flexibility in starting and stopping gas offtakes in line with the spark spread.

The market rules themselves can be a source of risk and will affect different technologies differently. For example, changes in electricity market rules that put an opportunity cost on unreliability of output have affected the cost of wind power in the United Kingdom. Similarly, price signals that encourage more efficient use of the electricity grid will also favour technologies that can locate to take advantage of these incentives.

---

11. IEA, 2001.

12. IEA, 2002b.

The costs of additional emissions controls, formerly passed directly on to consumers, must now also be considered as a risk to the profitability of power investments. Existing emissions controls on coal-fired plants include particulates and sulphur dioxide. Both coal and natural gas plants are covered by emissions controls on nitrogen oxides. However, future regulatory actions to lower allowable levels, or to introduce controls on other substances such as mercury, remain a risk for investors. Nuclear power plants are restricted in their emissions of radionuclides and may be subject to additional safety regulations.

Probably the greatest uncertainty for investors in new power plants will be controls on future carbon dioxide emissions. In the European Union, an emissions trading directive will be issued in 2003. Canada has also indicated that they will use emissions trading to control emissions from large stationary sources of carbon dioxide (CO_2). The unknown value of carbon emissions permits and the mechanism chosen to allocate permits will become a very large and potentially critical uncertainty in power generation investment. This uncertainty will grow in the future, particularly as future restrictions on levels of carbon dioxide emissions beyond the first commitment period of the Kyoto Protocol are unknown. For investment in fossil-fired generation, the price of permits will directly affect the profitability of power plants. The price of the permit is also expected to have a strong influence on the price of electricity and will further increase uncertainty about future electricity prices.

The risks associated with gaining approval to construct a new power plant also differ by technology. The risk is lower and the time span for the approval process is usually shortest for gas-fired power plants and small power plants such as fuel cells and photovoltaics. Although this risk already existed in regulated markets, the ability to pass through the approval costs to consumers is no longer automatic.

The important point for power generation is that the nature of the risks (the "risk profile") is different for different types of generation technology and fuels (Table 2). Thus, even when levelised costs are equivalent and technologies are commercially proven, different risk profiles of different technologies can influence the choice of power generation mix, the range of technologies offered, and the strategies for their development and operation.

Table 2

Qualitative Comparison of Generating Technology by Risk Characteristics

Technology	Unit Size	Lead Time	Capital Cost/kW	Operating Cost	Fuel Cost	CO_2 Emissions	Regulatory Risk
CCGT	Medium	Short	Low	Low	High	Medium	Low
Coal	Large	Long	High	Medium	Medium	High	High
Nuclear	Very large	Long	High	Medium	Low	Nil	High
Hydro	Very large	Long	Very high	Very low	Nil	Nil	High
Wind	Small	Short	High	Very low	Nil	Nil	Medium
Recip. Engine	Small	Very short	Low	Low	High	Medium	Medium
Fuel Cells	Small	Very short	Very high	Medium	High	Medium	Low
Photovoltaics	Very small	Very short	Very high	Very low	Nil	Nil	Low

Notes: distributed generation technologies are shaded. CO_2 emissions refer to emissions during combustion/reformation only.

Gas-fired technologies have characteristics that should be favourable under these conditions. The relatively low capital cost, short lead time, standardised design and, for some technologies, flexibility in operation provide significant advantages to investors. On the other hand, natural gas price uncertainty remains a large risk to the investor.

Nuclear power plants, by contrast, have a relatively low proportion of fuel and operating costs but high capital cost. Furthermore, economies of scale have tended to favour very large plants (1 000 MW and above) resulting in a relatively large capital commitment to a single construction project and hence associated investment risk. Newer designs are more flexible with regard to operations. The potential economic advantages of building smaller, more modular nuclear plants are also being explored by some nuclear power plant designers.

Coal power projects have also tended to become more capital-intensive to take advantage of economies of scale, to meet tighter environmental standards more economically, and to improve fuel efficiency. As with nuclear plants, lead and construction times for coal-fired power plants can be long.

Hydro projects come in all scales. Larger ones demand substantial lead time and are exposed to considerable risks during the construction phase as the length of the project can be subject to delays, the cost of borrowing can also change and increase the cost of the project. Usually there is no borrowing available in accordance with the amortisation time of a hydro project. The large economic potential of hydro has not been fully developed in some developing countries because of the very substantial risk premium resulting from the high sovereign risk. Operations by contrast can be highly flexible and able to take advantage of market conditions to optimise profitability. Long-term shifts and variations in rainfall patterns, e.g. due to climate change, remain another risk factor.

Of other renewables, solar and wind capacity are also capital-intensive. These plants have some very attractive low-risk characteristics, including very short lead times, no fuel costs or emissions, and low operating costs (hence little effect should these costs escalate). However, the variability of output of wind power reduces the value of the power produced. On the other hand, the fact that solar electricity from photovoltaics is produced at the point of consumption and during daylight hours, when prices are generally higher, increases the value of its electricity.

Reciprocating engines and fuel cells are two distributed generation technologies that use fossil fuels. Like photovoltaics, these distributed generation technologies have very short lead times and can be installed directly at the site of an electricity consumer. Their flexibility of use means that they can be operated during hours when power prices are favourable.

The competitiveness of reciprocating engines is thus dependent on the cost of delivered electricity that the distributed technology replaces. When fuel prices are low and electricity prices high, owners of these distributed generation technologies can produce their own electricity and reduce purchases from the electricity market. Electricity consumers that own generation facilities thus have a kind of "physical hedge" on the marketplace that allows them to cap the prices they pay. Reciprocating engines are also portable, i.e. they can be sold and moved to another location.

Quantifying Investment Risks in Power Generation

While identifying investment risks in power generation may be straightforward, investors in power generation attempt to understand the relative importance of different risks by quantifying them where possible. For the more important risks, it will be prudent to adopt risk management strategies that can cost-effectively reduce exposure to such risks.

Thus, estimating the profitability of an investment must rely on modelling, requiring knowledge of the future costs and the future revenues of the generating project and their variation. For a company with choice among generating options, with different lead times, different uncertainties in costs, a uniform methodology must be developed to compare technologies with different characteristics.

The levelised cost methodology, a widely accepted costing method for investments, has been a useful tool for investors and for overall economic analysis because it evaluated costs and energy production and discounted them to take account of the time value of money. It provided an objective basis on which to provide a comparison of different technologies, e.g. for baseload power generation. This approach has been used in the NEA/IEA study, *Projected Costs of Generating Electricity*, last updated in 1998[13]. This approach reflected the reality of long-term financing, passing on costs to the (captive) customers, known technology paradigms, a predictable place in the merit order, a strong increase in consumption and a short build-up time for selling the output of a new plant. The levelised cost approach involves:

- Developing estimates for all major cost components for a selection of generating technologies comprising:
  - Capital costs, including initial expenditures (as well as associated interest costs during the construction period), ongoing capital costs while the plant is operational, and decommissioning costs.
  - Operating and maintenance costs.
  - Fuel costs based on forecasts of fuel prices and fuel conversion efficiencies for the generating technology (and fuel waste disposal costs as applicable).

---

13. NEA/IEA, 1998.

- Estimating the average annual energy production from the power plant according to assumptions about technical availability.

- Discounting the stream of costs to estimate their present value according to an assumed discount rate (5% and 10% were used).

- Using the same discounting procedure to estimate the present value of the energy production.

- Taking the ratio of the costs and energy output to obtain a levelised cost of power production.

This discounted cash flow (DCF) approach remains useful for providing a comparison among power generation technologies. Power companies will apply DCF methodology based on an internal target for return on equity (the "hurdle rate") to make a decision whether to invest or not and to decide between different projects. To assess various risks, different scenarios or sensitivities will be calculated, which often give a good assessment of the risks involved.

However, in an electricity market, what matters to the investor is the profitability of the investment against the risk to the capital employed. Provided that the market is operating efficiently, the investors will make the choice of a generating technology that incorporates risks and is also the most economic choice available. Unfortunately, it is difficult for the levelised cost methodology to incorporate risks effectively. Thus it needs to be complemented by approaches that account for risks in future costs and revenues.

New financial techniques are becoming available that help quantify the impact of these risks on the costs of different options. Such assessments can help investors make better decisions. Investments with lower risk should have correspondingly lower "hurdle rates" for investment.

For example, a recent study carried out at the Massachusetts Institute of Technology[14] on the future of nuclear power presented an economic comparison of generating technologies using a methodology that accounted for risk. In its approach, higher returns on equity and a higher share of relatively costly equity in the capital investment were assumed

---

14. MIT, 2003.

for nuclear power investment compared to coal or natural gas. The analysis also included the effect of taxes, which also increases the effective return on equity required for all technologies.

The results of this analysis are summarised in Table 3. The base scenario found that nuclear power was more expensive than coal or natural gas by a very wide margin (USD 25 per MWh). Using the same input assumptions, one can also calculate levelised unit energy costs using the method in the NEA/IEA study, i.e. which applies the same discount rates to all technologies. In this case, the gap between nuclear and CCGT is much smaller, even at 10% real discount rate. A significant part of the difference between the estimates can be attributed to the higher perceived risk and hence higher hurdle rate employed for nuclear power rather than other technologies.

Another simple technique is to use a probabilistic assessment to look at a wide range of uncertainties in key risks, e.g. natural gas costs and electricity prices. The resulting distribution of outputs gives both an expected value and a range of probabilities that an investment would be profitable. The results of one such simulation, performed for the US Energy Information Administration, are illustrated in Figure 3 for an investment in a natural gas combined cycle plant[15]. An analysis that assumes certain fuel and electricity prices yields a positive net present value. By contrast, a probabilistic assessment shows that the investment would stand about an 83% chance of

Table 3

Comparison of Levelised Unit Energy Cost Estimates Using Different Methodologies (USD/MWh)

Technology	MIT Study Base Case	Levelised Cost at 5% Discount Rate	Levelised Cost at 10% Discount Rate
Nuclear	67	44	55
CCGT	41	44	45
Coal	42	33	40

Sources: MIT, 2003 and Secretariat analysis.

15. EIA, 2002.

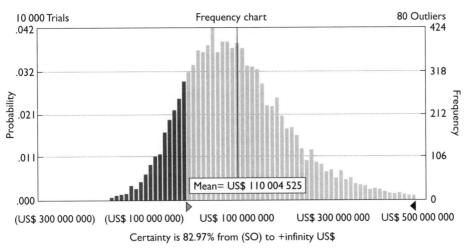

Figure 3

Net Present Value (NPV) Frequency Range for CCGT Investment

Source: Energy Information Administration.

being profitable over a 20-year period, given the forecast prices for electricity and natural gas and their uncertainty.

A second approach that can improve a discounted cash flow analysis is to discount costs and revenues at different rates according to their riskiness. Thus, for a power plant with more or less fixed costs but very uncertain revenues – the costs can be discounted at a low rate but revenues at a very high rate reflecting the uncertainty in future prices – the result can be an even higher effective discount rate. If a major cost component (such as fuel cost) is highly uncertain, its costs should be discounted at an even lower rate (the present value of costs is increased because of uncertainty).

Real Options and Investment in Peaking Plants

Estimating the profitability of peaking plants is a particularly difficult exercise in liberalised power markets. Peaking plants, by definition, depend on the high prices that appear over a relatively small number of hours to earn a return on the initial investment. The volatility of electricity and fuel prices makes prediction of the actual profits more difficult[16].

The fact that both fuel and power prices can be volatile can create not only risks, but also opportunities for the owners of peaking plants to make profits, producing electricity whenever the spark spread – the difference between the electricity price and the fuel cost – is favourable.

Discounted cash flow analyses tend to rely on single estimates of fuel and power prices, and thus underestimate profits that can be earned by peaking plants. A more accurate method needs to estimate how likely – in any hour – the favourable spark spread will occur. Sophisticated analytical approaches applying financial options methods can provide a means to estimate how many hours such plants are expected to operate, and the profits that can be expected from their operation.

A technique borrowed from financial options theory, known as real options, can be used to develop estimates of future uncertainty in prices given the observed volatility. By analysing the volatility of forward prices of electricity and key cost components (e.g. fuel costs), an estimate of the long-term uncertainty in profitability can be obtained[17]. It is this impact on long-term profitability than can influence investment.

Incorporation of uncertainty of fuel costs into estimates of profitability would appear to show the increasing importance of fuel cost uncertainty and volatility for profitability. However, these estimates must take account of at least two factors. In the short term, electricity and natural gas prices are sensitive to the supply and demand balance and have proven to be very volatile, a fact reflecting, among others, the relatively low short-term elasticity of demand for these commodities. In the long term, however, price movements are dictated by demand and supply fundamentals – e.g. when prices are high enough, new generating capacity is added (or new

---

16. *In considering the role of price risk in investment, it is useful to take account of the difference between the volatility of fuel or electricity prices and the uncertainty in these prices. Volatility is a measure of the degree of change in prices from one time period to the next. Electric power prices are highly volatile: prices can change from hour to hour by a factor of two or more and depend strongly on very specific factors such as the demand-supply balance or the price elasticity of demand. Volatility can be regarded as a measure of the rate of change of uncertainty in the price.*

17. *Geman, 2003.*

gas wells are drilled) to pull prices back towards long-run marginal costs of new generating capacity. This phenomenon of "mean reversion" means that power prices – and costs of major components of those prices such as fuel costs – are less uncertain than the short-term swings in these prices might imply.

The second factor is the extent to which natural gas prices are positively correlated with electricity prices. If an investor in a natural gas power plant can be assured that electricity prices will increase whenever natural gas prices increase (as a consequence of natural gas-fuelled generators being the marginal source of electricity), then the impact of natural gas prices on generation prices would be quite modest. Indeed, the EIA study cited above[18] assumed a positive correlation coefficient between electricity and gas prices of 0.88, based on its analysis of Henry Hub natural gas spot prices versus an average of electricity spot prices from 1999 to 2002.

The role of volatility can also be important depending on the type of plant. For the purposes of investment in baseload power generation, volatility is relatively unimportant compared to the expected average price level, as the plant is intended to be operating in nearly all hours. By contrast, a peaking plant will only be profitable to operate in a relatively small number of hours depending on a high enough spark spread in those hours. Fuel and power price volatilities create opportunities for the owners of peaking plants to make profits.

It is difficult to estimate the value of a peaking plant using discounted cash flow methods because these techniques tend to rely on single estimates of fuel and power prices. The very high uncertainty in price leads to discounting at very high rates and can lead to the conclusion that these plants are unprofitable. By relying on average conditions, however, these techniques underestimate the profit possibilities of those peaking plants to be employed only when the price of electricity is greater than the cost of producing it and when the plant is able to sell the gas if gas prices are high and electricity prices are relatively low. In other words, the value of the flexibility of a peaking plant tends to be underestimated.

---

18. EIA, 2002.

The real options method is a technique that can be used to estimate the value of a peaking plant, by valuing its ability to take advantage of volatile fuel and electricity prices[19]. In this method, the power plant itself is treated as a financial option, except that it is a "real" physical asset – a power plant – rather than a financial security. The value of the power plant then becomes a series of call options for each hour during which the power price or the fuel price can vary. The implicit assumption is that the power plant will operate in each and every hour in which it is profitable to do so, and will not operate in those hours in which it is not. Knowing the volatility in power and fuel prices helps quantify the uncertainty and the likelihood of profitability in any future hour.

Analysis of investment in a coal-fired mid-merit plant and a gas-fired peaking unit by using this technique suggests that both units have significant flexibility value that would actually be greater than the valuation suggested by the discounted cash flow approach. Results from this type of analysis suggest that prices paid for mid and peak power plants in the United States in the late 1990s can be better explained by real options approaches than by conventional discounted cash flow methods[20].

Value of Flexibility in Power Plant Development

Traditional investment analyses place limited emphasis on the timing of the investment versus market conditions. In these approaches, the value of developing a single large plant is considered rather than a series of smaller plants, although the smaller plant strategy might have an advantage, e.g. if the growth in demand for electricity turned out to be lower than expected. Without a method to quantify the value of this flexibility, the economies of scale evident in larger power plants (in terms of installed cost per kW) trump any concern about risks of adding capacity in larger units.

In energy markets, when future prices are uncertain, investors are aware of the potential value of proceeding incrementally in developing new

19. White and Poats, 2000.
20. Frayer and Uludere, 2001.

capacity. Quantitative methodologies that assess the value of being able to defer the decision of making part of the investment until market conditions become clearer have therefore been developed. Indeed, one of the early applications of the real options approach was to assess the value of phasing the development of oil fields versus a strategy of developing all at once[21].

Research to apply the same techniques to assess the flexibility value of different strategies for power generation project development is still at an early stage. One study has applied the real options method to estimate the value of developing wind power projects in stages, rather than all at once, in recognition of the inherent flexibility of smaller plants[22]. Another study examined the cost-effectiveness of developing an IGCC plant in phases, initially using natural gas as a fuel and thereby delaying the decision as to when to convert the plant to using gasified coal[23].

Despite these interesting academic results, the real options approach has achieved little acceptance by power generation investors to date. Calculating the real options value of a power plant has proven to be a less reliable indicator of value than financial options are in the stock market, for a variety of reasons. Unlike financial markets, forward markets for electricity and natural gas prices are not sufficiently liquid. The models must therefore rely on forecasts of future electricity and fuel prices. These forecasts, and the correlation between electricity and natural gas prices, are highly uncertain in light of changing volatility of these prices.

Summary

The reform of electricity and gas markets has led to major changes in the way decisions are taken on power sector investment. Opening the sector to competition has led to the internalisation of risk in investment decision-making. Investors now examine power generation options according to the different financial risks posed by the different technologies.

---

21. *McCormack and Sick, 2001.*

22. *Venetsanos et al., 2002.*

23. *Smeers et al., 2001.*

Given the long-term nature of electricity investments, investment decisions in baseload generating capacity are being made on the basis of long-term fundamentals rather than looking at short-term behaviour in the spot or forward electricity markets. Conventional discounted cash flow methods are still most often used. Nevertheless, investors are beginning to take account of differences in risk levels in assessing the likely profitability of different investments.

The current market preference for gas-fired power generation for baseload power generation in many OECD countries can be explained mainly by the perceived lower cost of gas-fired generation. The characteristics of the CCGT, its low capital cost, and its flexibility have added to its attractiveness. The importance of CCGT means that gas markets assume a greater importance than ever for power generation development. For governments, this means moving forward on liberalisation, and monitoring investment in both gas and electricity infrastructure.

The preference for gas-fired power generation does expose investors to increased fuel price risk. The creation or development of electricity and natural gas markets has led to a system where, in the absence of hedging possibilities, the risks of price development can no longer be managed, but must be assessed by probabilistic approaches.

The adequacy of investment in peaking generation remains an even more sensitive issue. The low numbers of hours of operation of peaking plants have led some to question whether markets can bring forward adequate peaking capacity. Low capital and high flexibility in operation are particularly important attributes in an attempt to value peaking capacity. While investors have long been aware of the qualitative benefits of flexibility in a liberalised market, new techniques have now been developed to quantify the value of flexibility. In particular, this research suggests that flexible peaking capacity may be much more profitable than traditional approaches would predict.

HEDGING RISK IN POWER GENERATION INVESTMENT

Introduction

Prior to liberalisation, investment in the power sector was a relatively low business risk and, in many cases, state ownership made access to debt capital relatively easy. Even for independent power producers, the availability of a long-term contract, which would pass the marketing risk through to a single buyer, made it possible to finance investment at a low risk premium.

The liberalisation of gas and electricity markets has changed the nature of corporations responsible for investment. Corporations are no longer directly responsible for ensuring adequate supply beyond their contractual obligations. As always, they remain responsible to their shareholders and they will invest only if their shareholders think it is profitable. Many state-owned companies have been privatised. Long-term purchase contracts for independent power producers are no longer common. Returns on investment are much more uncertain. The structure of electric utilities has also changed. Some countries have required firms to legally separate the network activities from the competitive and riskier businesses of generation and retail.

The role of the customer is also changing. Customers can choose the level of risk they wish to take with regard to the volatility of prices. They may also decide to invest in their own on-site power generation with the potential to sell surplus to other consumers. However, the ability of customers to react to price signals will depend on the type of customer. Furthermore, market opening in many jurisdictions is not yet open to household consumers.

Market liberalisation has also led to the opening of spot electricity markets in which producers could sell their output. The emergence of these markets encouraged the development of a new type of power plant investment – the so-called "merchant" power plant. A merchant power plant is a plant built where the output is sold at unregulated prices, either into electricity markets or through bilateral contracts. In the late 1990s, during a boom in power plant construction, finance was relatively easy to find for merchant power plants in US markets. However, thanks to a shift in market fundamentals (a slowing economy and rising natural gas prices) as well as particular events (California's electricity crisis, the bankruptcy of Enron), power prices and spark spreads fell dramatically, reducing the profitability of the new (mostly gas-fired) power plants. The aggregate loss in equity values for companies with merchant plant investments was measured in the hundreds of billions of dollars and a number of projects were cancelled[24]. The cost of capital for new plants in the United States has increased as the liquidity of electricity forward markets has greatly decreased[25]. As a consequence, it is currently difficult to obtain bank finance for new merchant power plant construction in the United States. Merchant power plant investment continues to occur in other jurisdictions, notably in Australia (see Chapter 4).

The risks associated with the merchant plant model have persuaded most investors to find mechanisms to hedge these risks. Financial hedging can use markets such as forward or futures markets to manage price risk. Contracts between producers and retailers or directly with consumers are another strategy that links the producer and consumer more directly. Finally, there are organisational strategies, mainly mergers, which are now emerging to deal with the risks associated with new investment or to respond to spark spread risk. Consumers may also hedge their risks by developing their own power plants.

Market Hedges

Financial hedging instruments such as futures and forward markets are important tools in the development of efficient electricity markets. Perhaps the best-developed electricity forward and futures markets exist in Nord Pool. The futures market Eltermin and options market (Eloption) have developed quite strongly in recent years, with trading volumes now significantly larger than the physical deliveries of 150 TWh/year. Eltermin provides financial contracts for power up to three years ahead. Figure 4

---

24. de Luze, 2003.
25. Joskow, 2003.

illustrates how electricity trade has developed in the Elspot market since 1998. Trade through Elspot has actually grown each year and now average trade is close to ten times physical deliveries. Eltermin and over-the-counter transactions have also grown (Figure 5) but fell off dramatically this past winter, a development attributable to the high electricity prices.

As is apparent from the figures, electricity trade in Nord Pool has taken several years to develop. Electricity market trade has also been growing in the United Kingdom and other parts of Europe. However, to date liquidity is still below a benchmark volume of 25 times of physical trade (Table 4). Low and falling liquidity is also reported for the Dutch market[26]. US markets are recovering from a post-Enron drop in liquidity.

The insufficiency of liquidity in financial markets for hedging electricity price risks means that investors seeking to hedge short-term price risks (or banks helping to finance these risks) cannot yet rely on these markets to help mitigate such risks. Theoretically, investors could construct a forward price curve to help them assess these investments and to hedge their income stream. But financial hedging instruments appear to have a much shorter time horizon than the term of the investment, leaving substantial residual risk. Indeed, it is unlikely that there would be sufficient

Table 4

Comparison of European Electricity Market Liquidity (as of April 2003)

Electricity Market	Ratio of Traded Amount/ Physical Demand
Powernext (France)	0.005
EEX (Germany)	2.5
Nord Pool	8.5
England and Wales	9
Liquidity benchmark	25

Source: Montfort, 2003.

---

26. Newbery et al., 2003.

Figure 4

Growth of Electricity Trade in Nordic Electricity Markets (1998-2003) – Elspot Market

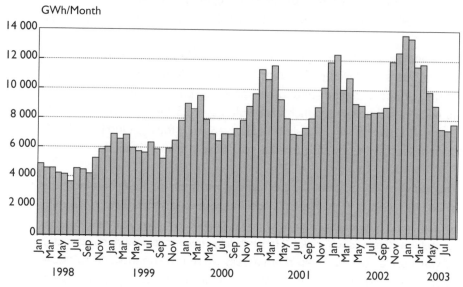

Source: Nord Pool.

demand for a long-term electricity futures contract to ever become a standard financial product.

Contract Hedges

If financial markets are not or not yet a practical tool for hedging against short-term risk and volatile prices, the common interest of consumers and producers in their desire to hedge against uncertain future electricity prices remains. Contract hedges between generators and consumers might therefore provide a more promising basis for hedging the risks associated with developing new power plants.

In fact, there appears to be relatively limited interest on the part of end-consumers in most countries to sign up for long-term contracts. Larger consumers are likely to be more interested in long-term arrangements in order to stabilise costs of inputs. In many markets, the existence of surplus

Figure 5

Growth of Electricity Trade in Nordic Electricity Markets (1998-2003) – Financial Markets

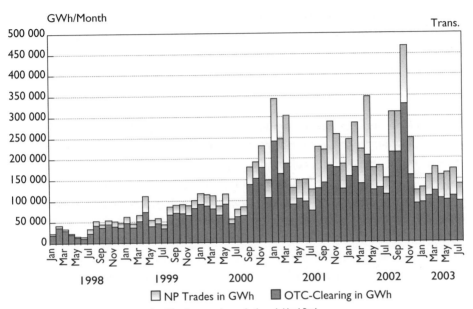

Note: OTC refers to over-the-counter trades. NP refers to trades made through Nord Pool.
Source: Nord Pool.

capacity and relatively low prices since liberalisation have discouraged long-term contracts because of differences between producers and consumers on future price levels. Yet, even as markets have tightened, particularly in Nord Pool, larger consumers continue to rely mainly on one to three-year contracts rather than contracts of longer term[27].

This leaves two other possibilities for longer-term contracting – either organisations of consumers (i.e. some form of consumer co-operative) or a contract with an electricity retailer with a large and relatively stable base of consumers. And, in fact, there are good examples of long-term contracts to finance new power generation investment.

The planned development of a new nuclear plant in Finland by the firm TVO is an example of a large consumer co-operative financing a new

27. Littlechild, 2002.

power plant. TVO is a long-existing co-operative consisting of both large electricity consumers and some municipal utility companies. TVO, which owns two nuclear power plants already in operation, sells electricity "at cost" to its investors in proportion to their contribution to the investment. With a guaranteed customer base who agrees to cover all costs, TVO expects to be able to finance future investment in a power plant at a very reasonable rate, making a nuclear plant its most cost-effective option[28]. In fact, it is a purchasing co-operative organising upstream integration as a joint venture.

The development of a new co-generation power plant in the Netherlands is a second example of a power plant financed by a 15-year power purchase agreement between the project developer (Intergen) and the retailer (Nuon)[29]. The prices in the first five years of the agreement are fixed by the contract (in turn backed by a gas supply agreement), with prices and quantities in years 6 to 15 shared between market and fixed price agreement[30]. The UK retailer Centrica has in the past year entered into a similar long-term agreement with Intergen for a UK gas-fired power plant in 2002[31] and more recently a four-year contract with British Energy[32].

However, such long-term arrangements by Centrica and other retailers are to date unusual. It can be expected that retailers will be less interested in signing long-term power purchase agreements given the ability of consumers to switch suppliers. This has raised concern that long-term contracting by retailers might be the missing link between the investors' desire for a long-term contract and some consumers' tendency to rely on short-term markets and spot prices. The US Federal Energy Regulatory Commission (FERC) had proposed that retailers in wholesale electricity markets in the United States be able to make arrangements in supply for up to three years in advance of real time. By including a forward contracting requirement in its proposals, the FERC hoped to

---

28. Santaholma, 2003.

29. Somerset, 2002.

30. The developer notes that finance was nonetheless difficult to obtain because of a strong lender aversion to the "merchant" component of the arrangement, and because of worsening financing conditions in general.

31. One major difference is that Centrica will supply the gas to the project. See Littlechild, 2002, p. 12.

32. British Energy, 2003.

encourage greater reliance on forward contracts rather than on the more volatile spot markets.

Another option for the consumer to hedge against shifts in power prices is to invest in on-site distributed generation. Falling capital costs for smaller power plants (particularly reciprocating engines or small turbines), opportunities for economic combined heat and power (CHP) generation, and a need for higher reliability increase the feasibility and attractiveness of this option. While successful in jurisdictions with high electricity prices such as Japan, the penetration of distributed generation technologies elsewhere in the OECD has been slowed by recent increases in natural gas prices and lower electricity prices, as well as institutional barriers[33].

Organisational Hedges

Recent experience with the merchant plant model has driven investors away from electricity sector investment. Investment banks, concerned by their losses in the United States and in some European markets, are now paying greater attention to companies with stable revenue flows and customer bases for future investments. In the United States, this means they are now attracted to lower risk options – regulated utility investments to finance new generating capacity.

However, where markets have already been liberalised, firms are restructuring themselves to mitigate the risks in such investments. In the United Kingdom, the generating companies that have been able to retain retail customers are better able to withstand falls in wholesale power prices caused by excess capacity, by having a sufficient retail base of customers under contract. All major generators in New Zealand have substantial customer bases, a process that was apparently accelerated in dry years as a result of price spikes[34].

---

33. IEA, 2002c.

34. "... there are incentives to under-hedge in the New Zealand market. In all but dry years (i.e. in most years) spot prices will be lower, and often much lower, than hedge prices (which build in a 'dry-year' insurance premium). This means that conservatively managed retailers, with a high level of hedge cover, are vulnerable to under-cutting by retailers buying mainly on spot, and who may exit the market in dry years." MEDNZ, 2001.

A strategy for companies making a significant investment in gas-fired generation to hedge against the risk of volatile gas prices is to acquire companies with upstream natural gas assets in order to hedge fuel cost

Table 5

World Top 15 Deals in Gas-Electricity Cross-Sectoral Mergers and Acquisitions

Name of Company Buyer-Seller (Country)	Date Effective (or Announced)	Deal Value (USD million)	Sector	Type
National Grid Group PLC Lattice Group PLC (United Kingdom)	Oct. 2002	18 440	Elec.-Gas	Midstream
Duke Power PanEnergy Corp. (United States)	Jun. 1997	7 667	Elec.-Gas	Upstream
Dominion Resources Inc Consolidated Natural Gas Co. (United States)	Jan. 2000	6 482	Elec.-Gas	Up, Mid, Downstream
Brooklyn Union Gas Co Long Island Lighting (United States)	May 1998	4 725	Gas-Elec.	Up, Mid, Downstream
DTE Energy Co MCN Energy Group Inc (United States)	May 2001	4 184	Elec.-Gas	Mid, Down
E.ON AG Ruhrgas AG (Germany)	May 2002	3 824	Elec.-Gas	Up, Mid, Downstream
Houston Industries Inc NorAm Energy Corp (United States)	Aug. 1997	3 649	Elec.-Gas	Up, Mid, Down
RWE AG – VEW AG (Germany)	Nov. 2000	3 432	Elec.-Gas	Up, Mid, Downstream
Fortum Corp (Finland) NYA Birka Energi (Sweden)	Feb. 2002	3 052	Gas-Elec.	Up, Mid, Downstream

Table 5

(continued)

Illinova Corp Dynergy Inc (United States)	Feb. 2000	2 852	Elec.-Gas	Up, Mid, Downstream
KeySpan Corp Eastern Enterprises (United States)	Nov. 2000	2 560	Elec.-Gas	Mid, Downstream
Dominion Resources Inc Louis Dreyfus Natural Gas (United States)	Nov. 2001	2 264	Elec.-Gas	Upstream, Downstream
Italenergia – Edison (Montedison) SpA (Italy)	Aug. 2001	2 139	Elec.-Gas	Mid, Downstream
Fortum Corp – Stora Enso Oyj Power Assets (Finland)	Jun. 2000	1 861	Gas-Elec.	Up, Midstream
Texas Utilities Co ENSERCH Corp (United States)	Aug. 1997	1 687	Elec.-Gas	Mid, Downstream

Source: Toh, 2003.

risks associated with gas-fired power generation[35]. Table 5 lists 15 large mergers since 1997 involving the gas and electricity sectors in OECD countries.

Gas-electricity convergence mergers may be attractive to investors for several reasons. The ability of the merged company to hedge the risks between natural gas production and gas-fired power generation has been a motivating factor in several mergers. The ability to generate power or arbitrage and sell gas, if that is more profitable, helps the merged company manage the price volatility in natural gas and electricity, in the absence of long-term contracts or liquid forward markets.

This form of "organisational hedging" is only one motivation for generation/retail or gas/electric mergers. More generally, mergers can be

---

35. Toh, 2003.

an effective way of gaining economic efficiency by increasing the efficiencies of the firms. However, there is also a danger that mergers could work against this objective if excessive market power were to lessen competition in the electricity and gas markets. Vertical reintegration or horizontal concentration can create market power that can be abused to reduce competition. Convergence mergers of gas suppliers with electric utilities can raise competitive concerns if it results in market power over the supply of fuel to a supplier. In the United States, the acquisition by the electric and gas utility CMS of two natural gas pipelines raised a concern over access to the CMS gas distribution system by shippers competing with CMS (e.g. shippers supplying power generators competing with CMS). The order approving the merger included conditions to ensure that these shippers would not be discriminated against[36].

Figure 6

Generating Capacity of the Largest EU-15 Utilities (2002)

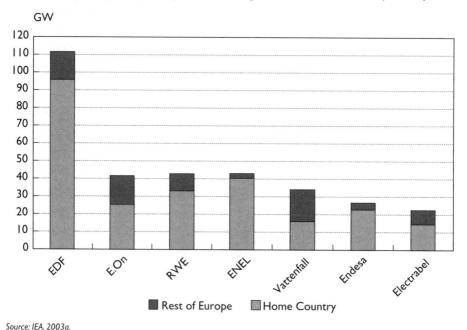

Source: IEA, 2003a.

36. Thompson, 1999.

Mergers are one mechanism to improve the prospects of stable cash flows as a source of finance for larger, capital-intensive investments. Higher equity financing is a way to cover more risky investment; it comes, however, at the price of higher financing costs. Indeed, the growth in power firms through mergers is, for this reason alone, not surprising. Mergers and acquisitions have led to the emergence, in Europe, of "The Seven Brothers" (EDF, E.On, RWE, ENEL, Vattenfall, Endesa, and Electrabel) that already hold a significant share of existing power generation assets (Figure 6), and are expected to contribute a significant portion of new investment from internal resources. Yet, the emergence of the size and scope of these firms has also raised concerns about concentration[37] of the industry.

Summary

Increased exposure to business and financial risk is also changing the structure of generating companies. Mergers among generators, between generators and producers, and between gas and electricity companies are all part of this response. This is increasing concerns about the potential impacts on competition in electricity markets and can be expected to continue to attract close regulatory attention. Finland's investment in a nuclear plant is exceptional, with large consumers of electricity willing to undertake the risks regarding nuclear plant investment because they expect to be able to obtain long-term financial benefits.

37. *Thomas, 2003.*

PRICE VOLATILITY, INVESTMENT AND GOVERNMENT INTERVENTION

Introduction

This chapter explores the role of government intervention in electricity markets in two dimensions. The first part of the chapter looks at price signals for investment in electricity markets and discusses the experience with high prices in some markets and the governments' response to these high prices. The second part of the chapter surveys different government policies to encourage investment in particular technologies, and the difficulty in ensuring that such investment in these technologies is carried out efficiently.

Price Signals

As a highly capital-intensive industry, a key sign of an efficiently functioning electricity supply industry is an efficient allocation of capital. In a market, prices are the key driver of investment decisions, as they signal potential rewards to investors. High prices relative to the cost of building new plants will signal the need for new investment. Low prices discourage investment.

As discussed in Chapter 2, the level of returns expected must be compared to the level of risk to which the investors are now exposed. Ultimately, investment in power generation is competing for capital with other industry investment opportunities.

Ideally, electricity markets should stimulate the right level of investments at the right time. The spot market price for electricity is the reference price to signal this investment. Even when electricity is traded under contract rather than through the spot market, the market price has become the basis for pricing electricity under contract.

The price level in the spot market varies greatly depending upon the supply-demand balance. When surplus capacity exists, it is expected that electricity markets would see prices well below long-run marginal costs (LRMC), not permitting marginal producers to recover any of their fixed costs.

In the long run, these prices below LRMC are not sustainable once there is a need for new investment in supply. Thus, prices will need to rise significantly to stimulate this investment. However, this price signal for investment is complicated by the unique combination of characteristics of electric power production. The inability to store electricity (in the way other commodities can be stored) means that plants can only produce for instantaneous consumption. Since there is a large variation in demand for electricity over a day or year, this means that significant amounts of capacity remain idle much of the time. Finally, the low demand-price elasticity of electricity means that when capacity begins to become scarce, prices can rise to very high levels, well above the long-run marginal costs (Figure 7).

In part because of the low demand-price elasticity, prices may be able to rise to very high levels over a relatively small number of hours to allow

Figure 7

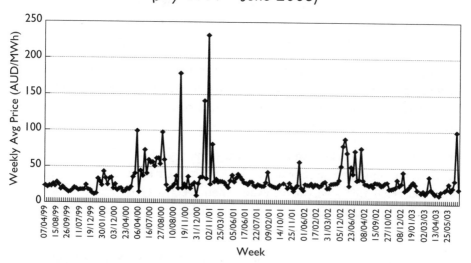

Spot Electricity Prices in the Victoria Market
(July 1999 – June 2003)

1 AUD = USD 0.59 (Q1 2003).
Source: NEMMCO data.

fixed costs of peaking plants to be recovered (see Table 6)[38]. Additional revenues from marginal generators (the peaking plants) can be earned from selling operating reserves in hours when they are successful in supplying the energy market. These revenue sources, in an energy-only market, should provide sufficient "scarcity rents" to provide sufficient revenues for investment in peaking plants. Payments during scarcity periods also contribute to the additional profits needed for baseload and midload capacity to cover their capital costs[39].

Investors anticipating these price spikes would make timely investments in new generating capacity. Investment would lead to a fall in electricity prices and the cycle would begin anew.

However, real electricity markets may not add capacity smoothly. Lags between price signals and construction of new plants may cause boom-and-bust cycles in generating capacity. Very hydro-dependent power systems may have large systemic risks e.g. due to variations in rainfall that may not easily be accommodated by investors or consumers.

Investment can also be strongly affected by government intervention or regulatory uncertainty. While spikes in the electricity price may occur in

Table 6

Prices Needed to Recoup Long-Run Marginal Cost in PJM in Top 5% of Hours by Load (USD/MWh)

LRMC	Average Price in Top 5% of Hours
35	225
40	294
45	363
50	432
55	500

Source: Hughes and Parece, 2002.

38. Hughes and Parece, 2002.
39. Hunt, 2002, Appendix E.

a well-functioning market to signal the need for investment in peaking capacity, they can also create significant hardship on power consumers who choose to be exposed to such prices. It may be argued that a rational, risk-adverse consumer will prefer to have a predictable price for electricity and will contract to obtain such a supply. Large customers in particular have been taking a variety of measures to provide greater pricing certainty. Even for large consumers, however there can be significant impacts. Large aluminum producers in the Pacific Northwest region of the United States are estimated to have cut 22 TWh of electricity demand during the electricity crisis of 2000-2001, as they determined it was more profitable to resell electricity than to produce aluminum. The crisis also precipitated a more permanent change as much of the aluminum industry in the region has closed permanently[40].

However, while larger consumers are more likely to be interested in contracting for supply, an argument can be made[41] that small consumers will be less inclined or even capable of doing so. Indeed, it is more likely that such consumers, having enjoyed years of relatively low-cost power, may lose interest in hedging themselves against future spikes. This will leave many consumers vulnerable to such price swings.

Another related question is the issue of whether wholesale market prices can be manipulated during times of scarcity. Two factors suggest governments should be concerned about the potential for market manipulation when supplies are scarce. First, many electricity markets today are rather concentrated, making it easier for generators with significant capacity shares to drive up prices by withholding capacity from the market. The second factor is the difficulty in proving that the abuse of market power is actually taking place. The experience of California demonstrated not only that such abuse of market power could occur, but that it can be difficult to prove that it is occurring. Indeed, it took well over a year before it became broadly established as one of a number of factors that contributed to high prices[42], long after price caps and other interventions had been implemented.

---

40. Only two of ten smelters remain in operation. See MacAuliffe, 2003.

41. Shuttleworth and Mackerron, 2002.

42. Joskow and Kahn, 2002.

There are now the ingredients for a political crisis related to electricity prices. Tightening electricity markets can produce high wholesale prices from time to time. However, large numbers of small consumers exposed to high prices will suffer hardship. A general rise in electricity bills among consumers is bound to be unpopular. Larger consumers may also find themselves exposed. There, the complaint will be about the impact of the higher prices (even if temporary) on jobs and competitiveness.

If consumers are accustomed to steady prices, or were promised falling prices as a result of the reform, they will blame the government for liberalising prices and place pressure on it to respond. Allegations of price manipulation will occur and will be difficult to disprove. The pressure for government or regulatory intervention will be very high.

The electricity "price crisis" described above is not simply a speculative possibility. In the past three years, there have been several electricity markets that have experienced high spot prices: those in California, Canada, Australia, Nord Pool countries and New Zealand (Table 7).

The causes of "price crises" are varied. Unlike in California, market power or bad market design does not appear to have played a significant role in the other cases. Price rises in Canada and Australia were driven principally by increases in demand for peak electricity (and by impacts of neighbouring markets). Those in New Zealand and Norway, with their hydropower dependence, were driven more by dry weather conditions. In all cases, as in California, governments were placed under considerable political pressure to respond to the concerns of consumers about prices and the security of supply.

These electricity "price crises" and the governments' responses to them are critical to understanding how electricity markets signal the need for new investment in generation. This chapter will briefly examine crises in Canada, Australia, New Zealand and Norway, and discuss how the government's response will affect future investment. The chapter concludes with a brief discussion of implications for government policy regarding the design of electricity markets.

Table 7

Markets Experiencing Electricity "Price Crises"

Juris-diction	Cause of Price Crisis	Duration	Government Response	Outcomes
Canada (Alberta)	High fuel prices, high electricity prices in neighbouring markets.	1/2001 – 3/2001	High retail price cap, rebates.	Market prices much lower than cap. New capacity entering market.
New Zealand	Tight energy supply due to low rainfall and concerns about availability of thermal fuels.	4/2001 – 7/2001	Government campaign for electricity savings.	6-10% savings in demand. Steps to improve market transparency, demand response and financial markets.
Australia (South Australia)	Tight capacity due to rapid growth.	1/2002 – 3/2002	Let market respond (but delayed retail liberalisation).	New capacity appeared quickly in response to high prices.
Nord Pool (Norway)	Tight energy supply due to low rainfall/cold winter.	12/2002 – 3/2003	Let market respond.	Large imports, significant demand response.
Canada (Ontario)	Demand growth, delay in capacity investment.	7/2002 – 7/2003	Low retail price cap, rebates. Government investment in peaking plant.	Wholesale prices high, no new private investment announced.
New Zealand	Tight energy supply due to low rainfall and concerns about availa-bility of thermal fuels.	4/2003 – 6/2003	Demand reduction, commission to acquire generating capacity for dry years.	Crisis averted through savings and increased rainfall.

Canada (Ontario and Alberta)

After a lengthy restructuring process, and the establishment of an independent regulator, the retail electricity market in Ontario was opened on 1 May 2002. All customers, regardless of size, had the right to choose their supplier of electricity. Customers not making this choice formally would be served by default through their local (usually a municipal) distributor who would buy spot electricity on their behalf. Electricity in Ontario is produced mainly from nuclear power (43%), coal and oil (25%), hydro (25%) and natural gas and other (7%). About three-quarters of the electricity is generated by provincially-owned Ontario Power Generation. Approximately 1.1 million residential consumers, about one-quarter of the total, had made arrangements for a fixed-price contract by the time the market was a few months old.

While prices during the spring were lower than regulated prices, a combination of an unusually hot summer and delays in bringing nuclear generating capacity back into service led to prices that were much higher than the government had anticipated. Combined with higher consumption, bills to Ontario consumers not covered by a fixed-price contract rose by approximately 30%. Voter dissatisfaction with the government over the market was very high.

As a result, in late 2002, the government passed legislation that froze prices for small consumers and institutional consumers (e.g. hospitals, schools, municipal buildings) at the level it was before the opening of the market (CAD 43/MWh[43]) until at least May 2006, compensated consumers for the additional amounts they had paid up to that point, froze rates for transmission and distribution of electricity, and empowered itself to change these rates previously determined by the regulator. Despite these changes, the wholesale market was left in place and the government is required to make up any difference between the wholesale cost of electricity and the frozen price.

These steps had a number of important short-term consequences: market prices remained high, and the government was now responsible for subsidising the prices paid for electricity. These subsidies cost CAD 550 million during the first 12 months of the operation of the market (Figure 8).

The government's action has also had an effect on electricity demand. Consumers covered by the price cap have less incentive to conserve electricity. This in turn has raised demand and the market price for electricity. It has also increased costs to the government (who must take

---

43. Equivalent to USD 28/MWh (1 CAD = 0.65 USD).

Figure 8

Wholesale Prices in the Ontario Electricity Market (May 2002 – April 2003)

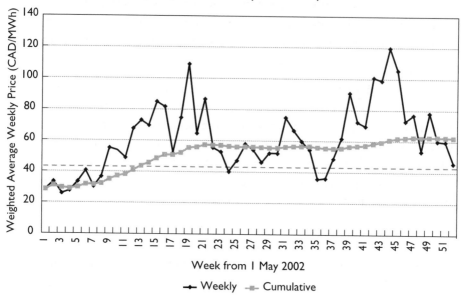

Week from 1 May 2002

→ Weekly ▪ Cumulative

1 CAD = 0.65 USD (Q1 2003).
Source: Independent Market Operator.

the spot price) and to those large consumers that had chosen to remain exposed to spot price. The continuing rise in demand has led the government to contract for an additional 270 MW of peak generating capacity to act as additional operating reserve[44]. The contracts, worth CAD 70 million, are for nine months only.

The high wholesale prices should begin to fall as capacity under construction at the time of the crisis is completed. However, no new projects have been proposed by the private sector since the government announced its shift in policy. The market operator has suggested the market will be short of peak capacity as early as 2005.

The government's temporary intervention to subsidise retail electricity prices has been set at a price far below that of the entry price for new generation (in the range of CAD 55 to 60/MWh). While the wholesale

---

44. Brennan and Spears, 2003.

market remains open and able to set prices freely, investors are more reluctant to move into the Ontario market because of the high political risks. As a consequence, prices in the wholesale market have to move even higher before new investment will occur. This leads to higher government subsidies and to increased risks of power shortages, which in turn leads to direct government intervention to add peaking capacity. Thus, the government finds itself paying for higher prices and for new supply. In October 2003, the new government announced its intention to raise the cap level.

Alberta has faced a similar situation at the time it opened its retail electricity market in January 2001, five years after a wholesale market had been established. Alberta relies on coal for around 70% of electricity generation and on natural gas for 26%. The retail market opened at the height of the California electricity crisis, when Western North American electricity and on natural gas prices were very high[45]. Alberta, as part of an interconnected market which includes California and the northwestern United States, also experienced very high market prices, with wholesale prices in 2000 (CAD 133/MWh) triple the value of the previous year and continuing into early 2001.

Most smaller customers were purchasing electricity through their local distributors who in turn were purchasing much of their needs at spot prices. These distributors applied to the regulator to raise retail electricity prices to pass through higher costs to customers.

The government's response was to establish a retail price cap on electricity and to pay for short-term relief through cash rebates. Unlike Ontario, the price cap was set at a relatively high level (CAD 110/MWh) although the impact on consumers was deferred until 2002 by requiring the utilities to delay collection of extra costs. Furthermore, the high cap was well above LRMC in order to preserve a signal for new investment. Wholesale prices in 2002 returned to 1999 levels. Investment in new generating capacity, which kept pace with growth in peak load, is continuing. A further 5 GW (approximately 40 % of existing capacity) is expected to be constructed in the period 2003-2006[46]. However, retail

---

45. AACE, 2002.

46. www.energy.gov.ab.ca

prices have risen considerably above pre-reform levels as utilities recovered the deferred costs from the wholesale price spike. Figure 9 shows that residential retail prices were actually lower than wholesale prices in 2000 but have subsequently risen as wholesale prices have fallen.

Figure 9

Retail Residential and Wholesale Prices in Alberta, Canada (1998-2002)

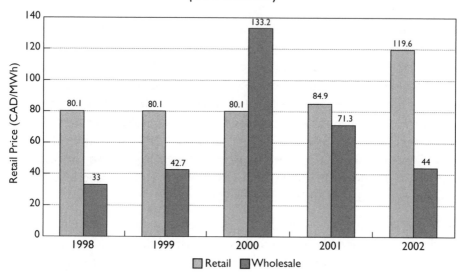

Note: Wholesale prices are annual averages of the daily average pool price. Retail prices for the city of Edmonton are based on a monthly consumption of 625 kWh, excluding tax.
Sources: Hydro Québec, 1998-2002 (retail) and Alberta Electricity System Operator (wholesale).

Australia (Victoria and South Australia)[47]

The Australian electricity supply industry, organised at the state level, is now becoming increasingly integrated on a national basis through the National Electricity Market (Figure 10). The market is dominated by coal-fired generation, although natural gas plays a significant role in South Australia (Table 8). Nevertheless, high growth (averaging 3% per annum in recent years) had led to tight demand and supply conditions and high spot

47. The discussion in this section is based on Cooke, 2003.

Figure 10

States in the Australian National Electricity Market

Table 8

Electricity Generation (GWh) in the National Market (2000/2001)

Type of fuel	NSW	VIC	QLD	SA	SMHEA	Total
Hydro	309	625	689	0	4 533	6 156
Black coal	63 358	0	42 208	0	0	105 566
Brown coal	0	48 465	0	4 479	0	52 945
Natural gas	1 019	881	2 128	6 104	0	10 131
Oil products	2	0	44	5	0	51
Total generation	64 688	49 971	45 069	10 588	4 533	174 849

SMHEA – Snowy Mountains Hydroelectric Authority.
Source: ESAA, 2003.

4 PRICE VOLATILITY, INVESTMENT AND GOVERNMENT INTERVENTION

prices in most states during peak periods (Figure 11). This section focuses on South Australia, where there has been a highly satisfactory investment response arising from a "price crisis". However, experience with government intervention in wholesale markets in Victoria is also described (see box).

In South Australia, high growth rates had led to dependence on imports from neighbouring Victoria. Tight conditions were reflected in the high average spot prices recorded during the initial period following market start (average spot price of around AUD 61/MWh in 1999-2000). High prices were accompanied by more frequent supply disruptions, particularly during extreme peaks in demand and reduced transmission capability with neighbouring Victoria. The government in South Australia decided not to intervene by capping market prices or by contracting for new investment. It did simplify its regulatory approval processes and decided to delay retail market opening for the smallest consumers.

Figure 11

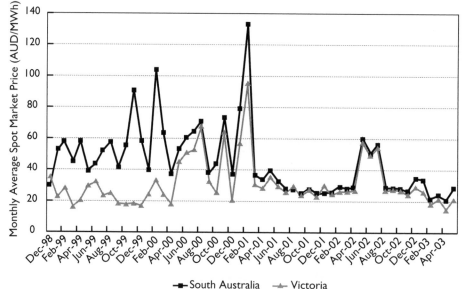

Monthly Average Spot Prices in Victoria/South Australia Electricity Markets (December 1998 to May 2003)

1 AUD = USD 0.59 (Q1 2003).
Source: NEMMCO data.

Box

Victoria: did government intervention delay investment?

In the state of Victoria, a strike at major generating facilities in January 2000 resulted in a shortfall of capacity at the annual peak. Under these extraordinary conditions, a cap mechanism on wholesale market prices known as the "Industrial Relations Force Majeure" (IRFM) was triggered. The IRFM capped prices paid to producers administratively rather than at the market price. The administrated cap, in place for approximately one month, produced an average price for Victoria of AUD 34/MWh versus an estimated "market" price of AUD 87/MWh.

The low administrated cap price left no economic incentive for short-run capacity or voluntary demand cuts to take place, beyond existing interruptible contracts. The combination of unexpected generation outages and extremely high summer temperatures saw the National Electricity Market operator (NEMMCO) begin to implement rotating power cuts on 3 February 2000. The Victoria government intervened by restricting electricity usage during peak hours, which avoided further rotating cuts. In fact, these restrictions were left in too long and, combined with the price caps, resulted in an export of electricity from Victoria to neighbouring states where prices were freely set.

Some investors have stated that certain investments in peak generating capacity were subsequently deferred as a consequence of the government's intervention in the market[48]. However, subsequent rises in spot prices the following year and anticipated continuing tight supply-demand balances encouraged new investment in peak capacity.

The consequence of the high prices in the South Australia market in these two years led to the addition of approximately 300 MW of peaking capacity in South Australia in addition to the 500 MW CCGT power station (Table 9). The new generating capacity of over 800 MW represented a 30% increase in existing capacity. The result was a quite dramatic decrease in peak prices and in the profitability of the peaking plants.

---

48. *Victoria, 2000.*

Table 9

Major Power Stations Placed in Service in South Australia

Plant	Capacity (MW)	In Service Period (phased)
Ladbroke Grove Gas Turbine (GT)	80	2000
Pelican Point Combined Cycle Gas Turbine	500	2000-2001
Quarantine GT	100	2001-2002
Hallett GT	180	2002

Source: NEMMCO data.

Understanding the impact of market prices on investment in South Australia requires some assumptions about the costs faced by new entrants. Table 10 summarises generating costs for these "model" new entrants used in the evaluation of an interconnector between South Australia and Victoria.

Table 10 implies that the short-run marginal costs for a gas peaking plant are AUD 40/MWh. Thus the number of hours above this level affects dramatically the cost-effectiveness of the peaking plant. If one makes the simplifying assumption that a gas turbine peaker operates during all of the

Table 10

Costs for "Model" New Entry Generating Technologies Serving South Australia

Technology	Capital Cost AUD/kW	Capital Cost (equivalent annual cost AUD/kW)	Short Run Marginal Cost (AUD/MWh)	Unit Size (MW)
Open Cycle Gas Turbine (GT)	500	80	40	50
Combined Cycle Gas Turbine (CCGT)	1 031	165	22	180
Brown coal (Victoria)	1 500	240	5	500

Source: NEMMCO, 2002.

hours when it is profitable to do so, one can calculate a simple estimate of the profitability of the peaking plant.

The entry of new capacity has had a dramatic effect not only on the average price, but on the distribution of power prices. In the years 1999 and 2000, prior to the entry of new peaking capacity, market prices were above AUD 40/MWh for about 43% of the time. In the two following years, thanks primarily to substantial new entry, this proportion of "peak-priced" power decreased to approximately 17% (Figure 12).

The entry of new peaking capacity was strictly on a market or merchant basis and thus was judged to be profitable by those entering. Their decision can indeed be justified on the basis of the expected profitability of the peaking plant. Table 11 shows the profitability of a peak, midload and baseload power plant with the short-run marginal costs of the entrants given in Table 10. The results suggest that a peaking plant in service in 1999 would have earned more than its entire capital investment in the first three years. Even an entrant at the beginning of 2001 (when much of the entry took place) would have earned satisfactory returns.

Figure 12

Distribution of South Australia Spot Power Prices (1999-2002)

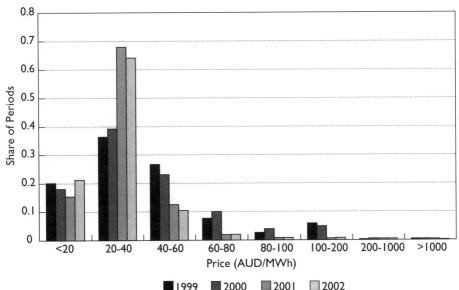

Source: IEA analysis from NEMMCO data.

Table 11 also shows the evolution of annual average wholesale prices in South Australia over the period. Prices decreased by approximately 35% between 1999 and 2002 largely as a consequence of the entry of new generating capacity.

Thus, the investment in a peaking plant appears to be justified by the prices obtainable in the market. One interesting question is the potential impact of a wholesale market price cap on the economics of peaking capacity. In the South Australian market, prices rose to the old price cap level of AUD 5 000/MWh (now raised to AUD 10 000/MWh) for a total of 5.5 hours in the four-year period. It is not therefore likely to have had much of an effect on the profitability of a peaking plant.

However, in other markets lower caps on wholesale market prices apply. In some US electricity markets, for example, a cap of USD 1 000 per MWh applies. If an equivalent cap (e.g. AUD 1 500/MWh) had been applied to the market in South Australia, the effect on the cost-effectiveness of the peaking plant would have been significant: a drop in the peaker's profits of about 24% on average over the four-year period and making the investment in peaking capacity significantly less attractive (Table 12). It should be noted that the drop in profitability of baseload or midload plant over the four-year period would have been identical (AUD 138/kW). However, as a percentage, the impact of the lower price

Table 11

Net Earnings of "Model" New Entrant Power Plants in South Australia (AUD/kW)

	1999	2000	2001	2002	Total	Capital Cost
Peaking (GT)	199	217	116	69	601	500
Midload (CCGT)	293	319	186	130	928	1 031
Baseload (brown coal)	433	456	325	266	1 480	1 500
Capacity factor of peaking plant	43%	43%	17%	15%		
Annual average wholesale price (AUD/MWh)	54.5	56.9	42.2	35.3		

Note: Brown coal plant is assumed to be constructed in Victoria.

Table 12

Impact of AUD 1 500/MWh Price Cap on Peaking Plant Profitability (AUD/kW)

	1999	2000	2001	2002	Total
Peaker (AUD 5 000/MWh cap)	199	217	116	69	601
Peaker (AUD 1 500/MWh cap)	159	171	79	54	463
Difference	40	46	37	15	138
Number of hours affected	28.5	29.5	24	12	94
Impact on annual average price (AUD/MWh)	– 4.5	– 5.9	– 4.2	– 1.7	

Source: IEA analysis.

cap is much less than for the peaker (10% for the baseload plant, about 15% for the midload) because of the much higher spread between the variable cost and the wholesale price.

Another interesting aspect of the lower cap is its effect on wholesale prices. In fact, the lower cap might be expected to reduce average prices by 10%, but only if investment took place at the same rate as under the higher cap. Lower profitability under a lower cap may well have resulted in a slower investment response and consequently higher prices in 2001/2002 than were actually obtained.

Therefore, one can conclude the following from the example in South Australia:

- A wholesale electricity market can produce prices sufficient to stimulate new entry of peaking capacity into that market.

- Wholesale price caps, where imposed, must not unduly erode the price incentive for efficient entry of new peaking plant.

New Zealand

New Zealand, with its heavy reliance on hydropower (64%) has one of the lowest electricity prices in the OECD. However, its high hydro dependence, coupled with its lack of interconnection with other countries, has created risks of a shortfall of electricity production capability when there is a lack of rainfall. Such "dry years" have tended to occur in quick succession, e.g. four times between 1942 and 1948 and five successive years in the 1970s.

Since the opening of its retail market in the 1990s, New Zealand has gone through two further droughts, in 2001 and again in 2003. In 2001, electricity prices soared through a combination of relatively low rainfall and colder than normal weather (Figure 13).

Wholesale prices increased ten times (from NZD 40 to 400/MWh[49]) causing hardship to some consumers who had not adequately hedged. One large retailer was forced to leave the market. The government

Figure 13

Monthly Averages of NZ Spot Electricity Prices
(August 1999 – July 2003)

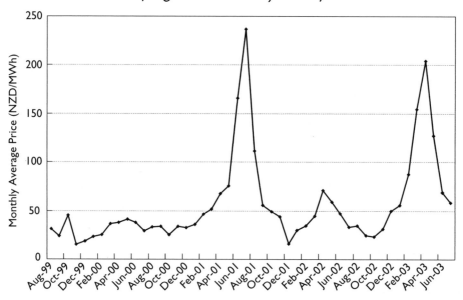

I NZD = USD 0.55.
Source: M-Co.

49. i.e. from USD 22/MWh to USD 220/MWh.

intervened through an energy conservation campaign that helped to avert supply shortfalls.

After the 2001 experience, the government of New Zealand reviewed the need to reform the market. It noted that buyers had the ability to hedge against high prices the previous summer but, perhaps lulled by a succession of rainy years and low prices, they had concluded that hedging was not necessary. The government undertook a number of measures to improve transparency in the marketplace, and suggested that further measures might be needed if effective retail competition did not develop.

Two years later, the electricity system went through a similar energy shortfall with prices beginning to rise in April 2003. The shortfall was caused by a prolonged period of low hydro inflows, and concerns about the availability of gas and coal for thermal generation. A successful energy conservation campaign combined with higher rainfall heading into the winter averted power shortages.

However, the government has concluded that the current electricity market does not provide enough incentive to invest in generating capacity that would provide sufficient supply in very dry years. The government was particularly concerned that some of the existing thermal generating capacity would be scrapped because of insufficient commercial incentives to keep it operating.

Its main policy proposal is to create an Electricity Commission to take reasonable steps to ensure security of supply even in a "1 in 60" dry year without the need to resort to an emergency conservation campaign[50]. The Commission will do this principally by contracting for reserve energy to be withheld from the market during normal years and made available only during dry years. The reserve energy would be offered into the market once the spot price begins to exceed a certain level and is expected to reduce price volatility. The government states that this policy should avoid the industrial production losses caused by the high spot prices as well as the public inconvenience associated with the energy savings campaigns.

---

50. MEDNZ, 2003.

Norway

Norway, which produces nearly all of its electricity from hydropower, has had an electricity market in operation since 1991. Electricity prices had generally fallen over the decade. The market in Norway has become increasingly integrated with its Nordic neighbours (Sweden, Finland and Denmark). Low prices have led to low levels of investment both in production capacity and in transmission grids. During wet years, Norway exports electricity to its neighbours and to other countries in continental Europe. In years of normal precipitation, however, imports of electricity have now become necessary. In dry years, imports combined with high prices to ration available production are necessary.

Very low precipitation levels in the autumn of 2002 led to very low reservoir levels and reduced energy generation capability. Furthermore, the weather in the winter of 2002/03 was colder than normal. As a consequence, electricity prices rose sharply in Norway this past winter. Market prices rose to record-high levels, and were far higher than the previous winters (Figure 14).

The short-term impact on retail electricity prices varied strongly by customer group. The very high spot electricity prices in the winter 2002/03 have led to proportionately larger impacts on household consumers. As a group, household consumers had the largest increases in electricity prices in both absolute and percentage terms. By contrast, the largest and most energy-intensive consumers had entered into contracts under fixed price arrangements covering 99% of their demand, and actually enjoyed a 32% price decrease compared to the same period the year before (Table 13).

The principal reason for the difference in short-term price impact can be explained by the relative share of fixed price contract arrangements by the different groups. The overwhelming majority of the household customers had chosen variable price rates, rather than being locked into a fixed price contract. By contrast, the majority of large energy-intensive consumers have relied more heavily on fixed price arrangements.

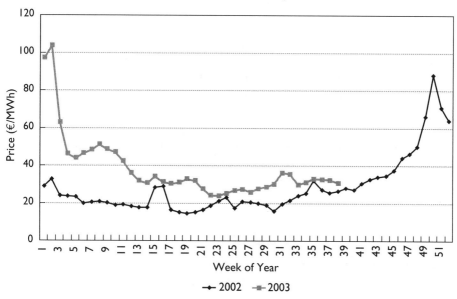

Figure 14

Nord Pool Weekly Averages of Spot Electricity Prices
(2003 vs. 2002)

Price (€/MWh) vs. Week of Year

—◆— 2002   —■— 2003

Source: Nord Pool.

Table 13

Changes in Retail Electricity Prices in Norway
(2003 Q1 vs. 2002 Q1)

Customer Group	Price Q1 2002 (ore/kWh)	Price Q1 2003 (ore/kWh)	Change (%)	Customers on Fixed-Price Contracts (%)
Households	23.7	62.4	131	7.8
Services	18.7	39.4	110	22.3
Industry (excluding energy-intensive)	18.1	31.4	73	55.1
Energy-intensive industry	16.8	11.3	−32	99.5*

Prices are exclusive of taxes. Exchange rate: 8.17 ore = € 0.01.
* Includes contracts not entered in the market.
Source: Statistics Norway.

The behaviour of the smaller consumers in Norway can partly be explained by comparing the variable price and the fixed price contracts in recent years. The variable rate contract offered on average a lower price compared to the fixed price contract – during the late 1990s (Figure 15). Even as variable price contracts became more expensive, most household consumers avoided fixed price contracts. Indeed the share of customers on fixed price contracts actually fell from 10% in 2002 to 7.8% in the first quarter of 2003, although the share of households on fixed price contracts doubled, to 16%, in the second quarter of 2003.

Government response to the crisis in Norway was aimed at increasing awareness of the problem and encouraging energy conservation. Spurred by high prices, the reduction in electricity consumption was significant, despite the cold winter.

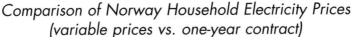

Figure 15

Comparison of Norway Household Electricity Prices (variable prices vs. one-year contract)

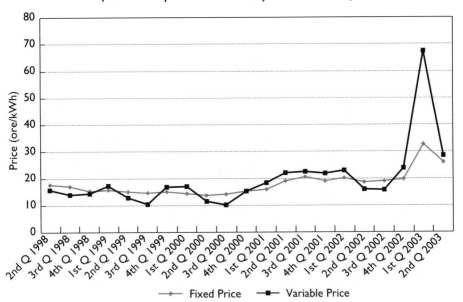

1 ore = 0.0012 euro.
Source: Statistics Norway.

Discussion of Implications for Governments

Drawing general lessons from government management of electricity "price crises" and its impact on investment is difficult given the rather different circumstances of each crisis and the relatively short period of time that has passed. Nevertheless, some observations can be made on the role that governments might play.

The experience in Australia, where consumption was growing by 33% during the ten years from 1990 to 2000 suggests that governments need to carefully consider the implications of their policies and subsequent actions on private investors that the reforms are attempting to attract. If investors expect that governments will intervene in wholesale markets to prevent prices from rising to sufficiently high levels to recover costs of peaking capacity, then attracting these investors will become more difficult and hence undermine reliability objectives. The experience in South Australia suggests that markets can respond to price signals and meet demand and reliability requirements where government policies are consistent with the development of efficient and sustainable electricity markets, and where they are implemented transparently and consistently.

The Canadian experience with retail price caps appears to be yielding two very different results in terms of investment. The Alberta market experience suggests that a sufficiently high cap on prices may not deter investment in new capacity. However, the recent experience in Ontario shows that actions by government to intervene with low price caps can deter investment. Indeed, such political intervention breaks the integrity of the market – by destroying incentives to invest and by creating moral hazard. If generators believe that customers will be protected by government intervention from spikes that are needed to recover fixed costs, then markets will fail to deliver new capacity.

This is not to suggest that price caps may never be needed in wholesale markets. When there is a demonstration of market power being exercised, as was seen in the California market, price caps may be needed as a temporary instrument to prevent excessive profits from being taken. However, such a measure should be transitional only, and should be phased out as quickly as other mechanisms to address market power, such as enhanced demand response, can be implemented[51]. Administered wholesale prices will also be needed under emergency conditions, e.g. as seen in Victoria in February 2000 or during the recovery of a power system following a system-wide blackout.

By contrast, the New Zealand situation presents quite unusual circumstances, because the combination of its heavy reliance on hydro resources and its lack of interconnection with other non-hydro systems makes it vulnerable to energy shortages that are difficult to predict. Having otherwise surplus capacity available for infrequent dry years does not appear to be economic.

The government's proposal to contract for reserve capacity that would be set aside from the market and be offered only during dry years would address this problem. The main difficulty with this proposal is the terms under which the capacity would be released to the market. The government has stated that it intends to release the capacity in the market only during times of shortage. It will, however, be difficult to define the level of shortage and the quantity to be released in a way that does not disrupt the behaviour of market participants. Disruption would be minimised if the capacity were only to be made available at very high prices. But there will be pressure on the government to release capacity to the market whenever prices rise. In this regard, the situation would be analogous to those pressures on IEA governments to release oil stocks to the market whenever oil prices rise.

In Norway, the government faced considerable dissatisfaction with high electricity prices. However, there were at least three factors that helped give the government greater confidence in relying on market mechanisms to resolve the crisis. First, there had been a long history of open electricity markets in Norway, and this had led to a better utilisation of generating capacity and lower electricity prices over several years. The fact that customers had already enjoyed several years of benefits increased confidence that the electricity markets do create benefits for end consumers. Second, the opening of the market internationally, thereby getting access to additional supplies from neighbouring countries,

---

51. See Kahn, 2002.

helped to reduce the risk that the market could be manipulated when capacity was tight. Finally, the existence of the international electricity market also meant that effective intervention by the Norwegian government would have to be co-ordinated with actions by the governments of the other countries served by this market. In fact, such co-ordinated discussions among Nordic ministers are carried out on a regular basis. This mechanism is much better suited to considered joint action rather than a short-term response.

Preventing Price Crises while Stimulating Investment

Governments reforming the electricity supply industry recognise that prices for power will need to increase substantially from time to time to stimulate new investment. As consumers are free to contract for new supply on the terms they choose, there will inevitably be significant groups of consumers who find a large rise in their bills. While governments may come under political pressure to intervene to lower prices, such intervention risks undermining investment.

How can governments avoid disrupting the market mechanism to stimulate new supply while avoiding the political consequences associated with high electricity prices? Two complementary strategies can be suggested. First, governments need to be assured that markets are effectively competitive, *i.e.* that high prices during tight markets are not the consequence of abuse of market power. The second is to attempt to find mechanisms that will reduce the volatility of prices without disrupting the use of market signals to invest.

Creating Effectively Competitive Markets

The importance of scarcity pricing to signal new investment in peaking capacity means that electricity markets need to function well when supplies are tight and not just at other times. Governments therefore must ensure their market reform policies can create workably competitive markets that are resistant to manipulation under these conditions.

The main elements of creating such markets have been discussed in *Competition in Electricity Markets* and other IEA reports. To be assured that electricity markets are not subject to manipulation whenever supplies are tight would particularly require:

- **Deconcentrated generation:** A sufficient number of generators competing to supply consumers and competing to supply the market during peak hours.

- **Market surveillance:** The ability to carefully watch market behaviour and, more importantly, to be able to take prompt action if market manipulation is suspected. The perceived slow response of the US Federal Energy Regulatory Commission at the time of the California crisis certainly underscores the need for the authority responsible for oversight to be able to act quickly.

Price-responsive Demand and Investment

Price behaviour during times of scarcity is important for new investment in peaking capacity. Ideally in a competitive market, prices should be determined by how much consumers value the electricity they consume and how much it costs to supply it. When capacity is adequate, the price is set at the marginal cost of supply and is far lower than the value all consumers place on electricity. Thus in markets with a large surplus of generating capacity, one should expect relatively little demand response – the electricity price is too low to make any response cost-effective.

By contrast, whenever capacity is scarce, the price should rise to a level until demand is reduced to a level that matches supply. In other words, electricity markets, like other commodity markets, rely on the demand side to set the wholesale price for electricity when capacity is scarce – to ensure that markets always clear (Figure 16).

However, experience has shown that the demand for electricity in tight electricity markets does not decrease appreciably when the price for electricity rises. In other words, the demand for electricity appears to be inelastic in the short term to the increases in price. The vertical line in Figure 16 illustrates this. As this figure might suggest, this means that, as available supply for electricity reaches its limits, prices can be expected to

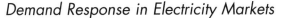

Figure 16

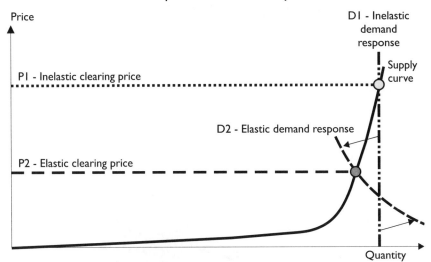

Demand Response in Electricity Markets

Source: IEA, 2003b.

rise quite dramatically. Furthermore, since demand and supply conditions change continuously, one can also expect prices to be volatile.

Figure 17 illustrates the pricing behaviour in the Ontario market over the first twelve months of operation (May 2002 – April 2003). The figure shows that while the average price appears to rise linearly with demand at lower demand, prices rise more quickly at higher demand and become more volatile, with prices in some hours over ten times the average price (CAD 62/MWh) over the period.

Thus, the low demand-price elasticity of electricity consumption will lead to high and volatile prices whenever supplies are tight. Low demand elasticity is partly the result of the special characteristic of electricity as a non-storable commodity that is consumed as it is produced. It also reflects, in part, the very high value that consumers place on a reliable flow of electricity – to be able to consume as much as they are able to whenever they wish – regardless of the cost.

However, not all customers or particular uses of electricity by particular customers require this near-continuous reliability that electricity systems

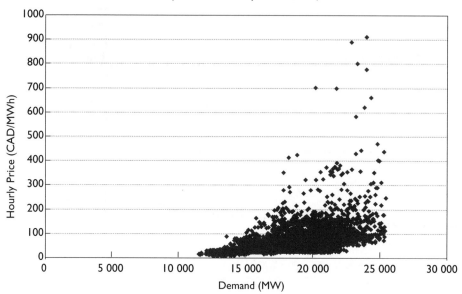

Figure 17

Scatter Plot of Prices vs. Demand in the Ontario Market
(May 2002 – April 2003)

Source: Ontario Independent Market Operator.

have been traditionally designed to provide. Certain industrial customers have long been willing, for a price, to reduce their demand (by stopping a single electricity-intensive process, for example) when requested for a limited period. Residential customers, while valuing overall reliability of their supply, have proven to be willing to curtail certain uses for a limited time (e.g. by turning off their water heaters) in response to some form of financial incentive. Thus, the value of electricity varies with each customer, depending on the end-use and on the particular customer's preferences and on the time of use.

There have also been limited capability and incentives for consumers to respond to prices in an organised way. First of all, nearly all consumers are able to consume electricity at all times and pay the bill later. Second, small consumers have been offered few price incentives to control their time of use of electricity. On the contrary, most have been exposed to regulated electricity tariffs that do not reflect the value of the electricity associated with the time of its use. Finally, the technology to monitor or manage electricity demand in real time (and hence measure and reward changes in consumption behaviour) was considered too expensive for demand response to be cost-effective for small consumers.

The short-term and long-term impacts of enhancing demand response on an electricity market are quite different though both are beneficial to the market's functioning. Enhancing the availability of price-responsive demand reduces the level of prices during peak periods. The immediate impact of increasing elasticity will be a transfer of revenue from producers generally (who will receive lower prices for peak electricity) to all consumers. Some percentages of these savings are the real economic benefit (lower cost of meeting electricity demand), but most of the impact will be what economists call a "rent transfer", meaning that consumers pay less money to producers for the same service without any improvement in economic efficiency.

In the short term, the impact of lower prices will be to encourage power producers to delay investments in new peak production. However, this delay in investment is temporary; it means that peak electricity demand is being met more cost-effectively through demand response than through an increase in supply. To avoid the disincentives for investment in peak generation that increased demand response would give, it is important that the focus be on increasing demand response in an economically efficient way[52].

Over the medium to long term, stronger elasticity means that electricity price volatility will be reduced and peaks in electricity prices will not be as high. However, the market will still signal the need for new capacity by spreading lower peaks over a larger number of hours[53].

Thus, the main long-term economic impacts are somewhat lower prices for electricity but, more importantly, less volatile prices. This will be beneficial for both consumers of electricity and producers as it makes

---

52. *Ruff, 2002.*
53. *See Ruff, 2002, p. 4.*

prices more predictable, easier to contract and thus should reduce risks and help the market function more effectively.

A related economic consequence of enhancing demand response is the reduced vulnerability of electricity markets to market manipulation. In a market where a single generator or a small number of generators are dominant, it is well known that generators can increase market prices e.g. by withholding generating capacity from the market when supplies are tight. Generally speaking, the fewer the number of firms, the greater this risk. In the case of so-called Cournot competition the average increase in prices above marginal cost is given by the following expression:

$$(Price - Marginal\ Cost)/Price = HHI/\varepsilon$$

where HHI (Hirschmann-Herfindahl Index) = sum of the squares of the market shares of each competitor

and ε = demand-price elasticity

This simple model, which is commonly employed in modelling competition in concentrated electricity markets, suggests that market power problems are more likely to arise in concentrated electricity markets with weak demand response. Both conditions apply in many electricity markets.

Conversely, increasing the demand-price elasticity can have the effect of reducing the ability of generators to manipulate markets[54]. In markets where institutional or other concerns might not permit a sufficient deconcentration of generation, measures to increase price-responsive demand can help to make electricity markets workably competitive.

In summary, a policy to enhance price-responsive demand can improve the functioning of electricity markets by enabling price to allocate supply when supply resources are scarce. Developing existing potential for price-responsive demand will lower electricity price peaks, reduce risks of market manipulation and, in the long run, could create more stable prices for generators and consumers[55]. This more stable environment will

---

54. Borenstein et al., 1998.

55. See IEA, 2003b.

encourage investment and reduce the risk of government intervention to address high spot market prices.

Capacity Mechanisms

Electricity market designers have attempted to deal with price volatility concerns through designing the markets to achieve new investment without high spot prices. Capacity mechanisms are intended to do this by placing obligations on retailers to acquire more than sufficient capacity to supply consumers. In the United States, requirements for capacity payments based on installed capacity are used in New York, New England, and PJM[56] markets. The Spanish electricity market also incorporates a capacity payment.

The US Federal Energy Regulatory Commission has proposed that regional wholesale electricity markets be responsible to ensure that there are adequate resources (including generation, transmission, energy efficiency and demand) available to meet peak demand for electricity in order to "promote long overdue investment and avoid over-reliance on the spot market auction"[57]. This proposal would have required retailers (known as load serving entities or LSEs) to arrange for sufficient supplies to meet peak demand plus a 12% reserve margin by contracting their expected needs up to 3 years in advance. LSEs that failed to satisfy the requirement would have been subject to penalties.

By encouraging forward contracting, the FERC is hoping to create a more stable environment for investment in generation than reliance on spot prices. The FERC proposals point out that a number of imperfections in today's US electricity markets, including caps on wholesale prices and the lack of price-responsive demand, make electricity markets vulnerable to underinvestment, particularly in peaking capacity. There is limited empirical information to support that contention since, overall, there has been plentiful investment (125 GW from 2000 to 2002, a capacity increase of 17%) that has left many markets oversupplied. Concerns about price volatility and its impact on consumers may be a prime

---

56. *A US electricity market encompassing most of the states of Pennsylvania, New Jersey, and Maryland.*

57. *FERC, 2002.*

motivating factor for consumers and for US regulators[58]. However, in current market conditions, providing a more stable environment for future investment must also be a consideration.

The use of capacity mechanisms elsewhere in OECD countries is limited. One reason for this being the existence of non-regulated alternatives to capacity mechanisms, including long-term bilateral contracts between generators and buyers of electricity, and financial contracts that help manage price volatility. In addition, a principal difficulty is that capacity mechanisms, in practice, may give a further advantage to incumbents. There may also be incentives in the short term for gaming the rules, for instance by manipulating availability of plants to increase revenue. Another potential shortcoming of capacity mechanisms is that they may discourage innovation and increase pollution by maintaining uneconomic existing power generating capacity.

The example from South Australia shows that a wholesale market can produce prices that are sufficient to stimulate new entry of peaking capacity into that market without a capacity mechanism. Not surprisingly, a major study prepared for the Council of Australian Governments examined the concept of imposing such capacity requirements and concluded that existing arrangements for capacity payments in other markets "have not generally met with success" and did not recommend implementing them for the Australian national market[59]. In fact, several other recent reviews have also examined the question of capacity payments in electricity markets. Reviews in Ireland[60], by Nordic ministers[61], and the UK White Paper on Energy Policy[62] have all reached the conclusion that capacity payment systems are not necessary to stimulate new investment.

Nevertheless, the existing imperfections in real electricity markets are quite significant. The risks of high electricity prices that might subsequently lead to government intervention may result in an even less

---

58. *Besser et al., 2002.*

59. *COAG, 2002.*

60. *CER, 2003.*

61. *Nordel, 2002.*

62. *DTI, 2003.*

desirable result than a capacity mechanism might entail. Conversely, the analysis above of the South Australian experience suggests that wholesale price caps, where imposed, might have to be set rather high (AUD 5 000/MWh) to attract adequate peaking capacity. Therefore, while the long-term emphasis must remain on improving electricity market functioning, including enhancement of price-responsive demand and sufficiently high price caps, interim measures to ensure adequate resources might still be worth considering.

Designing such a mechanism that encourages generation investment without price spikes and without the problems experienced by existing mechanisms will be difficult. Fixed capacity markets in the United States have had volatile payments for capacity, which is believed to have deterred investors from investing in peaking plant. It has been suggested that certain features of a successful mechanism would include: requiring retailers to contract for future needs (including the ability for their loads to be cut during periods of tight supply); evaluating the performance of these retailers during periods of tight supplies; and applying enforceable penalties on retailers that fail to comply with resource adequacy requirements (including financial guarantees to ensure the ability of the retailer to pay such penalties)[63].

In fact, the New York Independent System Operator (NYISO) has now introduced an additional capacity mechanism to encourage investment in peaking capacity. The NYISO has a capacity mechanism (ICAP) that requires retailers to contract for adequate amounts of capacity to serve their customers. While retailers already own or contract for a significant portion of capacity, short-run capacity needs could be acquired through an auction with the prices paid depending on the retailers' bid price for capacity. The NYISO concluded that the bidding produced a level of revenues that was both too low and too volatile to attract sufficient peaking capacity. The ISO has thus replaced its bid-based mechanism by a payment for short-term capacity obligations as a function of the estimated cost of new entry of peaking plant and the quantity of available capacity (Figure 18). The payment is set sufficiently high to attract new entry whenever available reserves are low and therefore to increase or

---

63. Joskow, 2003.

Figure 18

"Demand Curve" for Capacity Auction for New York ISO (New York City)

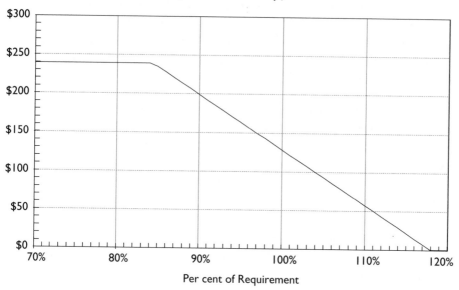

Per cent of Requirement

Source: NYISO, 2003.

decrease more smoothly than bid-based capacity auctions had done. An initial capacity auction in May 2003 attracted an additional 2 GW of capacity for peak load, largely through imports. A similar scheme is under consideration in New England.

It is much too early to pass judgement on the effectiveness of the NYISO scheme in attracting new peaking capacity to be constructed in the NY market, or on whether capacity acquired in this auction has been acquired in a cost-effective way. It should be pointed out that the auction is really intended to acquire the "balance" of capacity obligation, and if retailers can acquire this capacity more cost-effectively on their own, they can do so, reducing the quantity obtained from the capacity auction.

CONCLUSIONS AND RECOMMENDATIONS

The question of investment in power generation in electricity markets remains a sensitive issue in electricity market reform. Much of the focus has been on security of electricity supply, and on whether the overall level of investment in electricity markets has been satisfactory. Previous IEA work has shown that substantial investment in generating capacity has taken place and that OECD electricity markets generally provide reliable supply, the exception of California notwithstanding. However, it also concluded that the biggest challenges remain ahead – most reformed markets were reformed with excess generating capacity and are just beginning to approach their first major investment cycle.

This report has examined the ways investors adapt to reformed electricity markets. In particular, it reviews new analytical methods to assess risks, new mechanisms for financing investments and the consequences for the choice of generating technologies. The report has found that in view of the risks they are facing, companies in competitive markets will tend to favour more flexible technologies and this is consistent with the very high share of gas-fired power plants in global power plant orders.

The report has also described the recent experience of volatile prices in electricity markets and their impacts on consumers and particularly on government policies towards electricity reform.

Risk and its Influence on Power Generation Investment and Corporate Structure

Internalisation of business and financial risks has altered investment decision-making. The reform of electricity and gas markets has led to changes in the way decisions are taken on power sector investment by addressing the commercial risks of new investment. Internalisation of risk in investment decision-making has led investors to examine power generation options according to the different financial risks posed by the different technologies.

Uncertainties in future price levels tend to favour flexible, short lead-time technologies. Given the long-term nature of electricity investments, investment decisions are being made on the basis of long-term fundamentals rather than by looking at short-term behaviour in the spot or forward electricity markets. Nevertheless, new techniques have been developed to quantify these risks and opportunities associated with the volatility in electricity prices and are beginning to be applied and to influence investment in generation.

The current preference for gas-fired power generation in many countries can be explained in part by these new developments. The ability to add capacity quickly, to expand capacity at an existing power plant, or to switch fuels is becoming increasingly valued as investors look to technological developments to help them deal with uncertainty. Investments such as large hydro or nuclear plants, by contrast, bear a larger investment risk.

Nuclear plants can be financed in an electricity market, but it is much easier if customers share the risks. The decision of Finland's TVO company to proceed with the investment in a nuclear plant is the first by a company in a competitive electricity market. The structure of the investment is exceptional, however, with large consumers of electricity willing to take the risks of investing in a nuclear plant because they expect to be able to obtain the long-term financial benefits.

Because of the current economic downturn in the US electricity market, lenders look for strong companies with stable revenue flows and customer bases for future investments. Liberalisation has also affected the way power plants are financed. Early enthusiasm for the merchant power plant model, where power plants are financed without the security of regulated profits, has dissipated as a result of adverse investment experience in the United States.

Electricity companies are also growing in size as a means of mitigating risks and financing investment. The structure of generating companies is also changing to deal with increased exposure to business and financial risk. Mergers among generators, between generators and producers, and between gas and electricity companies, are all part of this response. However, this development is a cause of growing concern about the potential impacts on competition in electricity markets, and can be expected to continue to attract close regulatory attention.

Electricity Markets, Electricity Price Volatility and Investment

High prices, above long-run marginal costs show the need for additional investment. Price spikes in some US markets, in markets in Australia, have led to the development of new generating capacity. The price spikes in hydro-based systems, which tend to be constrained on energy rather than peak capacity, tend to be less dramatic but of longer duration than in capacity-constrained systems.

While electricity markets may be delivering adequate levels of investment, price spikes are testing government resolve to leave prices to markets. Concentration of electricity markets and concerns about the manipulation of prices in some markets, such as in California, make it difficult for a government or a regulatory body to determine if prices are reflecting scarcity or are the result of the exercise of market power. In some cases, particularly when smaller consumers are exposed to these price spikes, this has sparked government intervention in electricity markets.

Protection of consumers against high prices must be carefully designed to avoid disruption of the market. Intervention by governments in the electricity markets threatens to disrupt the market mechanisms and to discourage investors. Default supply options for small consumers should be chosen carefully, with an awareness of the risks involved. Price caps, if employed, should be set before spikes occur, and at sufficiently high levels. They should also be transitional measures until a more workably competitive market can be established.

The very high price volatility experienced in electricity markets is a direct consequence of the very low demand-price elasticity of electricity consumption, especially by small customers. There is considerable evidence that this elasticity is lower than it need be owing to the lack of ability and incentives for demand to respond to price. Enhancing demand response will reduce the extreme prices experienced during tight supply, in effect by spreading the price peaks over a larger number of hours. This will create a more stable environment for generation investment and should increase confidence that electricity markets can be used to ration capacity by price, ensuring that the supply of electricity remains reliable.

Addressing security of supply is central to investment signals. Sufficient investment should not be a problem in OECD countries since consumers place very high value on electricity and are able to pay prices that recover costs. The difficulty is really finding a model that properly values the security of the electricity supply. The old monopoly system provided more than sufficient investment and consequently was not efficient. A new system based on bilateral contracts between producers and consumers can also work to supply electricity reliably, but consumers need to value their security of supply. For large consumers, this is not a problem, but the issue for small consumers is less clear, since they may be less aware of the price risks. Governments have a role in making consumers aware of these risks.

As a consequence, the government's security of supply policy is tied up with its policies affecting new investment. Some measures can be taken that will remove obstacles to new investment, e.g. by streamlining approval of new generating plant.

However, mechanisms that intervene directly in electricity markets, such as capacity market mechanisms, can have much stronger effects on the cost of electricity. Several recent government reviews of capacity mechanisms have rejected their use because of their inefficiency and debatable effectiveness in stimulating new investment. Nevertheless, a well-designed capacity mechanism that requires retailers to have arranged adequate resources during peak periods might help provide incentives for retailers to acquire sufficient peak capacity (or to work with customers to have sufficient demand response).

Recommendations

Define clearly the government's role in electricity market reform and the terms of its involvement as precisely as possible. Attracting investment in power generation requires a clear market design, with predictable changes and no interference into the market or into the operation of the independent institutions established to implement the market reform. The government's role must be clearly set out both as the agent of the reforms and in its energy policy involvement once the market opens.

Recognise that electricity price fluctuations are intrinsic to well-functioning electricity markets. Allowing markets to signal the need for new investment in generation means that prices will go high on occasion. Governments need to anticipate that such fluctuations will occur and ensure that consumers are aware of price risks, and have options to mitigate these risks.

Develop demand response within electricity markets. Fluctuating spot electricity prices offer rewards as well as risks. The low price elasticity of electricity demand – especially for small customers – is at least partly due to the inability to reward consumers for adjusting their consumption when prices are high. Greater demand response in electricity markets is needed to help ensure that the markets are always able to clear, *i.e.* by rationing electricity supply according to price rather than through brownouts or blackouts. A stronger demand response will help mitigate market power in electricity markets and provide potential investors with more predictable prices and therefore decrease risks of investment.

Be prepared to detect and to act upon manipulation in wholesale electricity markets. In order to address concerns about manipulation, governments must ensure that wholesale electricity markets have monitoring mechanisms that can not only detect manipulation as it is occurring but also take prompt action to mitigate its impacts. This will reduce pressure on the government to respond, e.g. through direct price caps which could drive away needed investment.

Monitor adequacy of gas markets and investments. The preference of investors in some markets for CCGT for building new power generation capacity means that gas markets assume a greater importance than ever for power generation development. For governments, this means moving forward on liberalisation of the gas market in tandem with the electricity market, and monitoring the adequacy of investment in both gas and electric infrastructure.

BIBLIOGRAPHY

AACE, 2002.Report to the Alberta Minister of Energy, Alberta Advisory Council on Electricity, June.

Besser, J., J. Farr and S. Tierney, 2002. "The Political Economy of Long-term Generation Adequacy: Why an ICAP Mechanism is Needed as Part of Standard Market Design", *Electricity Journal*, August/September, pp. 53-62.

Borenstein, S., J. Bushnell and C. R. Knittel, 1998. Comments on the Use of Computer Models for Merger Analysis in the Electricity Industry, FERC Docket No. PL98-6-000, June.

Brennan R. and J. Spears, 2003. "Ontario Buys Brownout Insurance", *Toronto Star*, 4 June.

British Energy, 2003. *British Energy signs major supply deal with Centrica*, British Energy Press Release, 7 February.

CER, 2003. *Irish Electricity Market – Proposed Decision,* Commission for Energy Regulation, Ireland, 30 April.

COAG, 2002. *Towards a Truly National and Efficient Energy Market,* Council of Australian Governments, Energy Market Review Final Report, Canberra.

Cooke, D. 2003. "Investment and Reliability in the Australian National Electricity Market: A Perspective", *IEA/NEA Workshop on Power Generation Investment in Liberalised Electricity Markets*, Paris, 25-26 March.

de Luze G., 2003. "Investment in power generation: A banker's perspective", *IEA/NEA Workshop on Power Generation Investment in Liberalised Electricity Markets*, Paris, 25-26 March.

Deng, S-J, B. Johnson and A. Sogomonian, 2001. "Exotic electricity options and the valuation of electricity generation and transmission assets", *Decision Support Systems* 30, pp. 383-392.

DTI, 2003. *Our energy future – creating a low-carbon economy,* UK government White Paper, February.

EC, 2001. *Electricity Liberalisation Indicators in Europe*, Brussels, October.

EIA, 2002. *Derivatives and Risk Management in the Petroleum, Natural Gas and Electricity Industries*, US Energy Information Administration, October.

ESAA, 2003. *Electricity Australia 2002*, Electricity Supply Association of Australia, Sydney.

FERC, 2002. *Standard Market Design*, Notice of Proposed Rulemaking, US Federal Energy Regulatory Commission, Docket Number RM-01-12000, July 31.

Frayer J. and N. Uludere, 2001. "What is it Worth? Application of Real Options Theory to the Valuation of Generation Assets", *The Electricity Journal*, October, pp. 40-51.

Geman, H. 2003. "Towards a European Market of Electricity, Spot and Derivatives Trading", presentation to the IEA/NEA Workshop on Power Generation Investment, 25 March.

Hewitt, P. 2002. "Statement to Parliament by Patricia Hewitt, UK Secretary of State for Trade and Industry, 28 November 2002", www.dti.gov.uk

W.R. Hughes and A. Parece, 2002. *The Economics of Price Spikes in Deregulated Power Markets*, Charles River Associates, www.crai.com

Hunt, S. 2002. *Making Competition Work in Electricity*, John Wiley & Sons, New York.

Hydro Québec, 1998-2002. *Comparison of Electricity Prices in Major North American Cities*, Hydro Quebec (editions 1998-2002).

IEA, 1994. *Electricity Supply Industry: Structure, Ownership and Regulation in OECD Countries*, International Energy Agency, Paris.

IEA, 1999. *Electricity Reform: Power Generating Costs and Investment*, International Energy Agency, Paris.

IEA 2001, *World Energy Outlook 2001 Insights – Assessing Today's Supplies to Fuel Tomorrow's Growth*, International Energy Agency, Paris.

IEA, 2002a. *Security of Supply in Electricity Markets: Evidence and Policy Issues*, International Energy Agency, Paris.

IEA 2002b, *World Energy Outlook 2002,* International Energy Agency, Paris.

IEA, 2002c. *Distributed Generation in Liberalised Electricity Markets,* International Energy Agency, Paris, p. 63.

IEA, 2003a. *World Energy Investment Outlook,* International Energy Agency, Paris.

IEA, 2003b. *The Power to Choose: Demand Response in Liberalised Electricity Markets,* International Energy Agency, Paris.

Joskow, P., 2003. *The Difficult Transition to Competitive Electricity Markets in the US,* CMI Working Paper 28.

Joskow P. and E. Kahn, 2002. "A Quantitative Analysis of Pricing Behaviour in California's Wholesale Electricity Market in the Summer of 2000", *The Energy Journal,* Vol. 23, No. 4, pp. 1-35.

Kahn, A., 2002. "The Adequacy of Prospective Returns on Generation Investments under Price Control Mechanisms", *The Electricity Journal,* Vol. 15, Issue 2, March, pp. 37-46.

Littlechild, S., 2002. *Competition in Retail Electricity Supply,* CMI Working Paper 9.

MacAuliffe, P., 2003. "NW United States Aluminum Industry Response to High Electricity Prices – or how the Aluminum Industry Saved the West", *Saving Electricity in a Hurry Workshop,* IEA, Paris, 20 June.

McCormack J. and G. Sick, 2001. "Valuing PUD Reserves: A Practical Application of Real Option Techniques", *Journal of Applied Corporate Finance,* Winter, pp. 8-13.

MEDNZ, 2001. *Electricity Post Winter Review,* Ministry of Economic Development, New Zealand.

MEDNZ, 2003. *Discussion Paper – Reserve Generation,* Ministry of Economic Development, 20 May.

MIT, 2003. *The Future of Nuclear Power,* An Interdisciplinary MIT Study, July.

Montfort, O., 2003. Presentation to "Liquidity in European Energy Trading", *Eurelectric Fifth Energy Trading Day Workshop,* Brussels, 28 April.

NEA/IEA, 1998. *Projected Costs of Generating Electricity, Update 1998,* Nuclear Energy Agency, International Energy Agency, Paris.

Newbery, D., 2000. *Privatization, Restructuring, and Regulation of Network Utilities,* MIT Press.

Newbery, D., N. Von der Fehr, E. Van Damme, 2003. *Liquidity in the Dutch Wholesale Electricity Market,* report by the Dutch Market Surveillance Committee, The Hague, 14 May.

Nordel, 2002. *Action Plan: Peak Production Capability and Peak Load in the Nordic Electricity Market,* Nordic Council of Ministers and Nordel, October 29.

NYISO, 2003. "NYISO Demand Curve for the NYCA Installed Capacity Market", presentation to the Harvard Electricity Policy Group, May 21.

Ruff, L.E., 2002. *Economic Principles of Demand Response in Electricity,* prepared for the Edison Electric Institute, Washington DC, October.

Santaholma, J., 2003. "Nuclear Power Investment, Case Finland", Presentation to the *IEA/NEA Workshop on Power Generation Investment,* Paris, 25 March.

Shuttleworth G. and G. Mackerron, 2002. *Guidance and Commitment: Persuading the Private Sector to Meet the Aims of Energy Policy,* report for Power Gen prepared by NERA, December 17.

Smeers, Y., L. Bolle and O. Squilbin, 2001. *Coal Options: Evaluation of Coal-based Power Generation in an Uncertain Context,* Belgian Federal Office for Scientific, Technical and Cultural Affairs, Report D/2001/1191/66.

Somerset, M. 2002. "Lessons Learned from an IPP", *Converging Gas and Power Markets,* Amsterdam, December.

Thomas, S. 2003. "The Seven Brothers", *Energy Policy* 31 (2003) 393-403.

Thompson, M.W. 1999. *Prepared Statement of the Federal Trade Commission Before the Committee on the Judiciary United States House of Representatives,* July 28.

Toh, K-H 2003. "The Impact of Convergence of the Gas and Electricity Industries: Trends and Policy Implications", IEA Working Paper, April.

Venetsanos, K., P. Angelopolou and T. Tsoutos, "Renewable Energy Project Appraisal Under Uncertainty: the case of wind energy exploitation within a changing energy market environment", *Energy Policy* (30) 293-307.

Victoria, 2000. *Security of Supply Task Force Report*, Victoria Department of Natural Resources and Environment, September.

White, D. and R. Poats, 2000. "The Role of Volatility Value in Power Plant Financing", *Journal of Project Finance*, Summer, pp. 23-31.

ORDER FORM

IEA BOOKS

Fax: +33 (0)1 40 57 65 59
E-mail: books@iea.org
www.iea.org/books

INTERNATIONAL ENERGY AGENCY

9, rue de la Fédération
F-75739 Paris Cedex 15

I would like to order the following publications

PUBLICATIONS	ISBN	QTY	PRICE	TOTAL
☐ **Power Generation Investment in Electricity Markets**	92-64-10556-5		€75	
☐ The Power to Choose - Demand Response in Liberalised Electricity Markets	92-64-10503-4		€75	
☐ World Energy Investment Outlook - 2003 Insights	92-64-01906-5		€150	
☐ Cool Appliances - Policy Strategies for Energy Efficient Homes	92-64-19661-7		€75	
☐ Creating Markets for Energy Technologies	92-64-09963-8		€75	
☐ Energy Policies of IEA Countries - 2003 Review (Compendium)	92-64-01480-2		€120	
☐ Energy Labels and Standards	92-64-17691-8		Free PDF	
☐ Dealing with Climate Change - Policies and Measures in IEA Member Countries	92-64-19841-5		€100	
			TOTAL	

DELIVERY DETAILS

Name _____ Organisation _____

Address _____

_____

Country _____ Postcode _____

Telephone _____ E-mail _____

PAYMENT DETAILS

☐ I enclose a cheque payable to IEA Publications for the sum of $ _____ or € _____

☐ Please debit my credit card (tick choice). ☐ Mastercard ☐ VISA ☐ American Express

Card no: └─┴─┴─┴─┴─┴─┴─┴─┴─┴─┴─┴─┴─┴─┴─┘

Expiry date: └─┴─┴─┴─┴─┘ Signature: _____

OECD PARIS CENTRE
Tel: (+33-01) 45 24 81 67
Fax: (+33-01) 49 10 42 76
E-mail: distribution@oecd.org

OECD BONN CENTRE
Tel: (+49-228) 959 12 15
Fax: (+49-228) 959 12 18
E-mail: bonn.contact@oecd.org

OECD MEXICO CENTRE
Tel: (+52-5) 280 12 09
Fax: (+52-5) 280 04 80
E-mail: mexico.contact@oecd.org

You can also send your order to your nearest OECD sales point or through the OECD online services:
www.oecd.org/ bookshop

OECD TOKYO CENTRE
Tel: (+81-3) 3586 2016
Fax: (+81-3) 3584 7929
E-mail: center@oecdtokyo.org

OECD WASHINGTON CENTER
Tel: (+1-202) 785-6323
Toll-free number for orders:
(+1-800) 456-6323
Fax: (+1-202) 785-0350
E-mail: washington.contact@oecd.org

IEA Publications, 9, rue de la Fédération, 75739 Paris Cedex 15
Printed in France by Jouve
(61 2003 30 1 P1) ISBN 92-64-1055-65 2003